Literature & Writing Connections

How to Make Books with Children Series

How to Make Books with Children, Literature & Writing Connections is about using literature as a resource for learning. Each of the 39 book-making projects include:

- step-by-step directions and patterns for making a book

- a list of current literature that connects with the book

- writing topics and projects that can be used to fill the pages of the book

- classroom activities that provide hands-on experiences related to the topic

How to Use This Book

- Extend story time and units of study.
  Read stories to discover more about a topic or an author's style. Then respond to this new information by doing activities, writing, and then creating a book to record your learnings and ideas.

- Provide patterns for cross-age projects.
  Peer tutors and buddy classes will enjoy working on these projects together.

- Create a classroom library.
  Create dozens of different books for your classroom library featuring your own students as authors.

EMC 777

Evan-Moor ®
EDUCATIONAL PUBLISHERS
Helping Children Learn since 1979

Authors: Jill Norris
              Joy Evans
Editor: Marilyn Evans
Illustrator: Cindy Davis
Desktop: Cheryl Puckett

Congratulations on your purchase of some of the finest teaching materials in the world.

For information about other Evan-Moor products,
call 1-800-777-4362 or FAX 1-800-777-4332.
Visit our Web site www.evan-moor.com
for additional product information.

Table of Contents

Pop-Up Book Binding

Paper Cover: Pop-up books generate lots of student interest. Students love to read the stories again and again to share the excitment of seeing the pop-up revealed. Follow these steps for easy, successful binding:

1 Glue each of the pages together. Press firmly and allow to dry.

2 Fold the cover paper in half. Lay the glued pop-up pages in the folder. Apply glue to the top pop-up page. Press the folder closed.

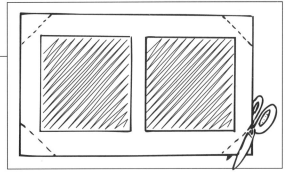

Flip the folder over. And apply glue to the inside back cover of the pop-up book. Close the folder and press firmly.

Cloth or Wallpaper Cover: Cardboard covered with cloth or wallpaper may be used to create sturdy and impressive covers for student pop-up books.

Cut two pieces of cardboard about two inches (5 cm) larger than the story pages. Place the cardboard on a piece of cloth cut slightly larger than the cover. Leave an appropriate amount of space between the cardboard pieces for the spine.

2 Miter the corners of the fabric. Brush diluted white glue onto the fabric border and fold over onto the cardboard.

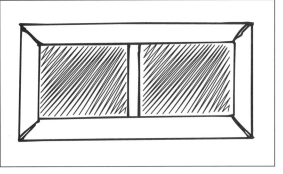

Lay the pop-up book inside the cover. Brush glue on the top page. Close the cover and press firmly. Turn the cover over and open to apply glue to last pop-up page. Close the cover and press firmly again. Set aside to dry.

Hinged Binding

A hinged binding is appropriate if the book contains many pages and you want to use tagboard or another heavy material for the cover. The hinged book creates a book cover that opens easily and stands up to many readings.

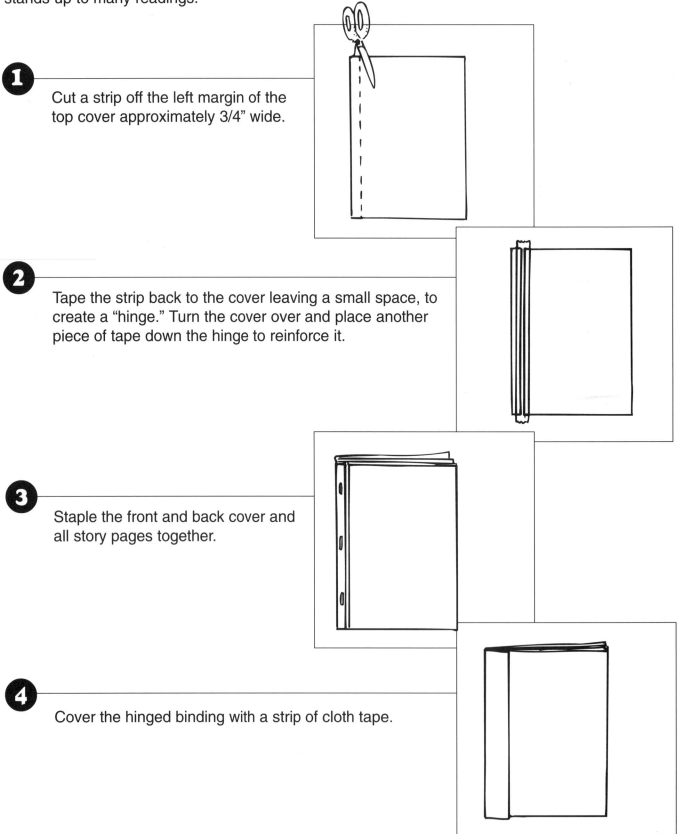

1 Cut a strip off the left margin of the top cover approximately 3/4" wide.

2 Tape the strip back to the cover leaving a small space, to create a "hinge." Turn the cover over and place another piece of tape down the hinge to reinforce it.

3 Staple the front and back cover and all story pages together.

4 Cover the hinged binding with a strip of cloth tape.

The Mitten

A Shape Book

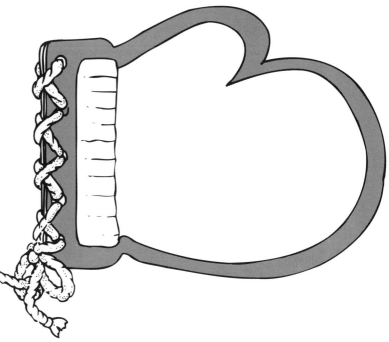

Materials

Class book:
- 2 sheets of 9" x 12" (20 x 30.5 cm) colored construction paper
- a copy of the mitten pattern on page 8
- student writing paper
- yarn
- hole punch, scissors
- glue, felt pens

Individual books:

Reproduce the pattern on page 8 for each student to color, cut, and use as a cover for an original story.

1

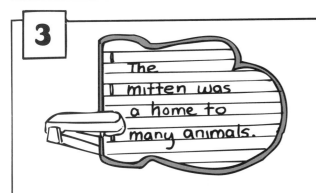

Decorate and cut out the pattern. Glue it to one of the pieces of construction paper.

2

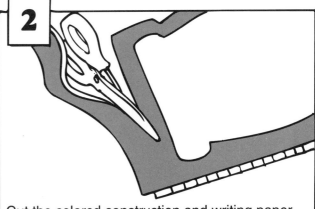

Cut the colored construction and writing paper to match the shape of the pattern.

3

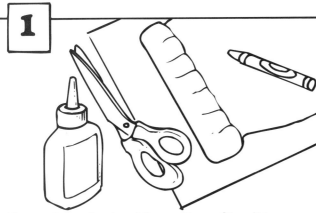

After students complete their stories, staple their papers to the back cover.

4

Place all layers together. Punch five holes and thread the yarn. Tie a bow, then knot the ends.

Literature Connections

***The Mystery of the Missing Red Mitten* by Steven Kellogg; Dial Books, 1974.**

When a little boy loses his mitten on a snowy day, he retraces his steps and finds the missing mitten in a heartwarming spot.

These three books retell the folktale of a lost mitten that is used as a home for many different animals.

***The Woodcutter's Mitten* by Loek Koopmans; Crocodile Books, 1990.**

***The Mitten* by Alvin R. Tresselt; Lothrop, Lee & Shepard, 1964.**

***The Mitten: An Old Ukrainian Folktale* by Jan Brett; G.P. Putnam's Sons, 1989.**

Writing Connections

A Mystery

Who took the missing Mitten?
Write a tale solving the mystery. Be sure to leave clues for your reader.

Writing Descriptions

Describe a mitten.
Write so that readers can see pictures of the mitten in their heads. Include details like its color, material, texture, and size.

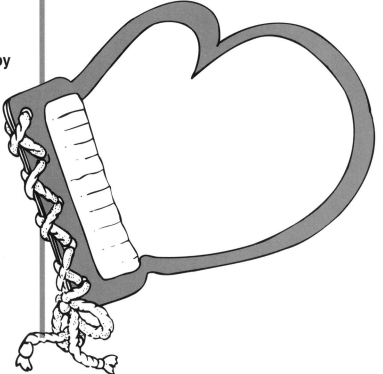

On a cold, wintry day with frost in the air
My fuzzy new mittens are just right to wear.
They keep my fingers snugly warm.
A shield against the fierce snow storm.

Jill Norris

 How to Make Books with Children EMC 777

Something More to Do...

Compare and Contrast Story Versions

1. Read several versions of the mitten folktale with your class.

2. Make a chart and record information to compare the retellings:
   • Whose mitten was lost?
   • Where was it lost?
   • What did it look like?
   • How was it lost?
   • What animals used it for a home?
   • What happened to the mitten in the end?

3. Write a new class or individual mitten story.
   • Begin by filling in the chart for a new story:
     Whose mitten will be lost?
     What will it look like?
     How and where will it be lost? etc.
   • Then write the story.

| The Mitten | |
Tresselt	Brett
What: yellow mitten	white mitten
Where: in woods	near house
Animals: mouse, frog, owl, rabbit, fox, wolf, boar, bear, cricket	mole, rabbit, hedgehog, owl, badger, fox, bear, mouse

More Writing Ideas

1. Older students may focus on using descriptive language that describes the animals and their bulging home.

"A chattering squirrel with a bristling tail spotted the lumpy mitten and peered inside."

2. Younger students might create a simple add-on book.

One

1

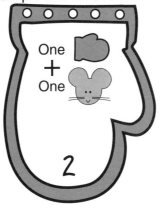

One
+
One

2

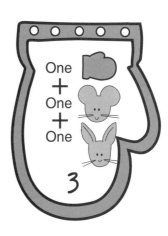

One
+
One
+
One

3

How to Make Books with Children EMC 777

The Cat

A Shape Book

Materials

Class book:

- 2 sheets of 12" x 18" (30.5 x 45.5 cm) colored construction paper
- the cat head pattern on page 11
- student writing paper
- 2 paper fasteners
- hole punch, scissors
- glue, felt pens

Individual books:

Reproduce the pattern on page 12 for each student to color, cut, and use as a cover for an original story.

1

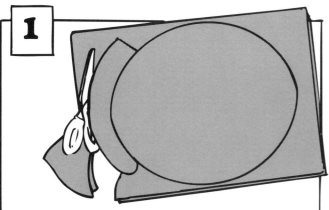

Cut two bodies and one tail from the colored paper.

2

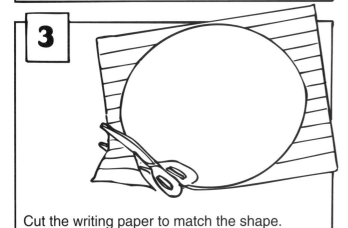

Cut and glue the cat's head. Draw in the cat's legs and paws.

3

Cut the writing paper to match the shape.

4

Punch holes and fasten the finished stories together with the paper fasteners. Attach the tail with the top fastener.

Literature Connections

Millions of Cats **by Wanda Gag; Coward-McCann, 1928.**

A charming old book about a woman who wants a cat.

Counting on Calico **by Phyllis Limbacher Tildes; Charlesbridge, 1995.**

A calico cat provides opportunities for practicing counting.

Moses the Kitten **by James Herriot; St. Martin's Press, 1984.**

An orphaned kitten is nursed back to health.

My Cat Jack **by Patricia Casey; Candlewick Press, 1994.**

A close-up look at the day-to-day activities of a pet cat.

Raining Cats and Dogs **by Jane Yolen; Harcourt Brace & Company, 1993.**

A series of parallel poems about cats and dogs.

Rich Cat, Poor Cat **by Bernard Waber; Scholastic, 1963.**

The lifestyles of several different cats are compared and contrasted in this book.

Writing Connections

Cat Ad

Write an advertisement for cats. What are the best things about a cat? Why should you own one?

The Cat Who Could Talk

Imagine that your cat suddenly starts talking. What would it say? What would you do?

The Cat's Journey

Many cats have traveled long distances to be with their human families. Write about a journey taken by a cat.

> **My kitten has a motor**
> **It hums beneath her fur.**
> **When she feels safe and loved,**
> **She starts it up. PURR, PURR!**
>
> *Jill Norris*

Millions of Cats Mural

1. Paint a long, green hill across the board.

2. Add a heading—"hundreds of cats, thousands of cats, millions and billions and trillions of cats".

3. Have each student make a folded paper cat to pin to the hill.

Folded Paper Cat:
- Fold a 6" x 9" black piece of paper.
- Cut out a scoop.
- Make one scoop the head.
- Make the other scoop the tail.

Hundreds of cats, thousands of cats, millions and billions and trillions of cats

12

The Chicken

A Shape Book

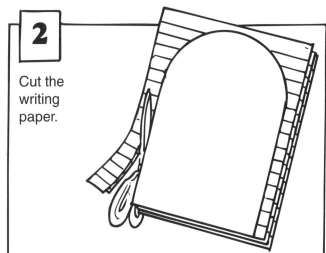

Materials

Class book:

- 2 sheets of 9" x 12" (20 x 30.5 cm) red construction paper
- scraps of colored construction paper
- 2 paper fasteners
- student writing paper
- two buttons
- scissors, hole punch
- glue, felt pens

Individual books:

Reproduce the pattern on page 16 for each student to color, cut, and use as a cover for an individual story.

1

Cut the red construction paper.

2

Cut the writing paper.

3

Cut the paper scraps to create the details. Glue them on the cover. Glue on the buttons for eyes.

4

Assemble all the stories. Punch holes through all layers and secure with the paper fasteners.

Literature Connections

Chester the Chick by Jane Burton;
Random House, 1988.

Text and color photographs chronicle a chick's
first year of life.

The Chick's Trick by Jeni Bassett;
Cobblehill Books, 1995.

Two hens insist that each has the best chick.

Gemma and the Baby Chick by Antonia
Barber; Scholastic, 1992.

Gemma helps to save a chick that is slow to
hatch.

Something to Crow About by Megan
Halsey; Dial Books, 1990.

Two chicks who look just the same find out how
different they are when one begins to lay eggs
and the other starts to crow.

Too Many Chickens by Paulette
Bourgeois; Little, Brown, 1990.

A teacher and her class accept a dozen eggs,
and then they begin to hatch.

Writing Connections

Little Chick's First Adventure

Write about what happened to the chick after it
hatched from its egg.

Chick Talk

Use only sound words and illustrations to tell a
story.

Not Enough Room

The chicken house is exploding with too many
chicks. What can Farmer John do?

TAP!
TAP!
TAP!
  Insistent pecks

CHIRP!
CHIRP!
CHIRP!
  Audible peeps

CRACK!
CRACK!
CRACK!
  Egg shell wrecks

CHEEP!
CHEEP!
CHEEP!
  Tired chick sleeps

Jill Norris

Something More to Do...

Chicken Little

1. Read or tell the tale of *Chicken Little*.

2. Have your students act out the events in the story or create a set of puppets to tell the tale.

3. Have students rewrite Chicken Little's story in their own words. Change the animals that Chicken Little meets. Change Chicken Little's destination.

4. Dramatize the new story, too.

Chicken Little Puppet

Paste the pattern on page 16 to a paper bag.

Here are some chick patterns to use as you wish!

How to Make Books with Children EMC 777

The Moon
A Shape Book

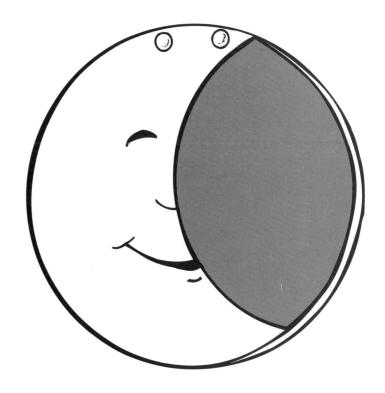

Materials

Class book:

- yellow tagboard
- 1 sheet of 12" x 18" (30.5 x 45.5 cm) blue construction paper
- 1 12" (30.5 cm) circle template
- 2 paper fasteners
- student writing paper
- hole punch, scissors
- glue, felt pens

Individual books:

Reproduce the pattern on page 20 for each student to color, cut, and use as a cover for an original story.

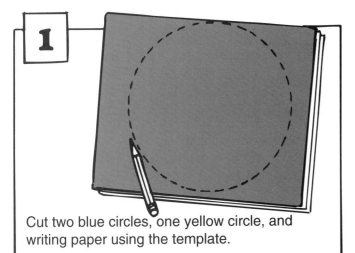

1 Cut two blue circles, one yellow circle, and writing paper using the template.

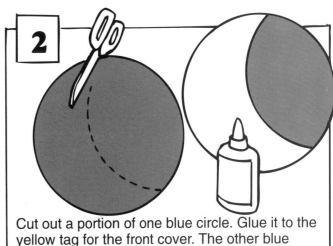

2 Cut out a portion of one blue circle. Glue it to the yellow tag for the front cover. The other blue circle is the back cover.

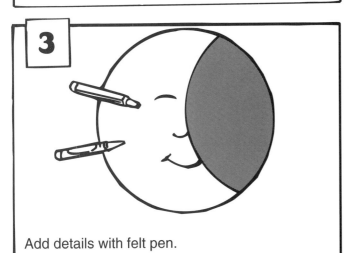

3 Add details with felt pen.

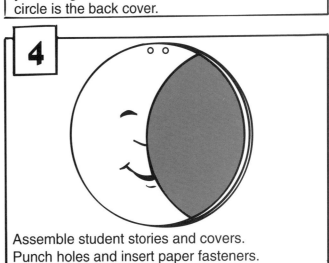

4 Assemble student stories and covers. Punch holes and insert paper fasteners.

17

Literature Connections

Moonhorse by Mary Pope Osborne; Alfred A. Knopf, 1991.

A winged horse takes a child on a journey across the night sky.

Moongame and **Mooncake** by Frank Asch; Scholastic, 1983 - 84.

Bear carries on a one-sided friendship with Moon.

Moon Jump: A Cowntdown by Paula Brown; Viking, 1993.

Ten cows participate in a contest to jump the moon.

Moon Mother by Ed Young; Willa Perlman, 1993.

In this Native American creation tale, the moon is the mother of man.

Moonsong Lullaby by Jamake Highwater; Lothrop, Lee & Shepard, 1981.

Photographs of the moon moving across the sky describe the night.

The Night Is an Animal by Candace Whitman; Farrar Straus Giroux, 1995.

In this bedtime metaphor, night is compared to an animal that travels across the earth.

What Rhymes with Moon? by Jane Yolen; Philomel Books, 1993.

A collection of nineteen poems about the moon.

Writing Connections

A Lullaby

Write a lullaby about the moon.

The Night Sky

Use similes and metaphors to describe the night sky.

Off to the Moon

What would you find if you were suddenly transported to the moon?

Peek-a-boo moon
In the night sky,
Shine down on me
As you go by.

Jill Norris

Something More to Do...

Make a Moon Phases Log

Provide your students with a calendar form for the month. As a homework project, assign them the task of viewing the moon nightly and drawing what they see in the calendar box for that day. (Choose a month where the weather is likely to be cooperative!)

Throughout the month, take time to discuss the observations being made. At the end of the month, students are to bring their calendars to school. Discuss their observations and label the drawings with the names of the phases.

Background for the Teacher

As the moon travels in orbit around the earth, different amounts of its lit surface are visible to us. These changes are called the **phases of the moon**. In one complete revolution around the earth—29 1/2 days or a lunar month—the moon passes through all of its phases.

As the amount of lighted surface that is seen grows larger, the moon is **waxing**. As the amount of lighted surface grows smaller, the moon is **waning**.

A Description of a Complete Revolution

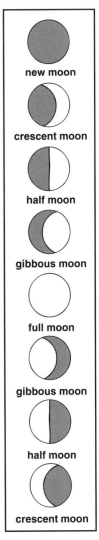

new moon

crescent moon

half moon

gibbous moon

full moon

gibbous moon

half moon

crescent moon

- The moon is between the earth and the sun and the moon cannot be seen at all. This is called the **new moon**.

- About one or two days later, a little of the lighted side of the moon can be seen. This is the **crescent moon**.

- About a week after the new moon, one half of the lighted side of the moon can be seen. This is called the **first quarter** or **half moon**.

- A few days later, almost all of the moon's lighted side can be seen. This phase is called the **gibbous moon**.

- About two weeks after the new moon, all of the lighted side of the moon can be seen. This phase is called the **full moon**. The earth is between the moon and the sun during this phase. The moon has made one half of a complete revolution around the earth.

- About one or two days after the full moon, the amount of lighted side that is seen grows smaller. A **gibbous moon** is seen from earth.

- About one week after the full moon, only one half of the moon's lighted side can be seen on earth. This phase is call the **last quarter** or **half moon**.

- After the last quarter, the moon wanes until it is a **crescent moon** again (also called an **old moon**.)

- About one week after the last quarter, the moon has completed its revolution around the earth and is back in its original position as a **new moon**.

19   How to Make Books with Children EMC 777

20   How to Make Books with Children EMC 777

The Pig

A Shape Book

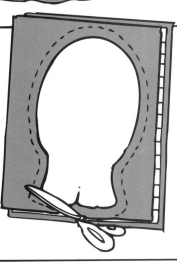

Materials

Class book:

- patterns on pages 23 and 24
- 9" x 12" (20 x 30.5 cm) construction paper
- a 2" (5 cm) square of cardboard
- a pipe cleaner
- hole punch, scissors
- glue, felt pens

Individual books:

Reproduce the patterns on pages 23 and 24 for each student. Color, cut and assemble the two pieces to create a cover for an original story.

1

Color and cut out the patterns.

2

Glue pig's body pattern to one of the construction paper sheets. Put both pieces of construction paper and writing paper together and cut around the shape.

3

Glue the cardboard in the center of the pattern. Glue the head pattern on top.

4

Assemble all parts and punch holes. Secure with the pipe cleaner. Curl the extra around a pencil.

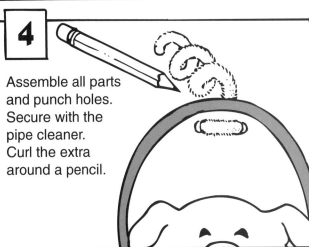

How to Make Books with Children EMC 777

Literature Connections

Annabel **by Janice Boland; Dial Books, 1993.**

Annabel doesn't want to be a pig anymore, so she tries out some other farm jobs.

The Book of Pigericks **by Arnold Lobel; Harper & Row, 1983.**

This book is a collection of silly limericks about pigs.

Little Pink Pig **by Pat Hutchins; Greenwillow, 1994.**

Mother can't find Little Pink Pig to put him to bed.

Millie and the Mudhole **by Valerie Reddix; Lothrop, Lee & Shepard, 1992.**

Millie, the pig, thinks that she knows everything there is to know about mud.

Pigs Aplenty, Pigs Galore! **by David McPhail; Dutton Children's Books, 1993.**

Pigs invade a house and have a wonderful party.

A Pile of Pigs **by Judith Ross Enderle and Stephanie Gordan Tessler; Bell Books, 1993.**

The pigs make a pyramid to see what the cows are doing.

Writing Connections

Pigs at Play

How are the pigs having fun? Rolling in the mud, grunting a merry tune...?

The Purple Piglet

What happens when the newborn piglet turns out to be bright purple?

All About Pigs

Organize all you know about pigs into paragraphs for a nonfiction pig report.

**Resting in a cool mud bath,
Rooting in the trough for treats,
The lazy pigs fill all their days
Snoozing and searching for "eats."**

Jill Norris

Something More to Do...

A Pig Poem

Practice rhyming by creating a nonsense poem about pigs.

1. Begin by thinking of rhyming words—big, dig, fig, gig, jig, rig, twig, wig...

2. Use these rhyming words to tell things a pig might "do." doing jigs, eating figs...

3. Follow the format shown at right:

Pigs, Pigs, Pigs

doing jigs,

making digs,

eating figs,

growing "bigs,"

Pigs, Pigs, Pigs

How to Make Books with Children EMC 777

The School Bus

A Shape Book

Materials

Class book:

- yellow tagboard
- writing paper
- 2 squares of 3" (7.5 cm) black tagboard
- bus patterns on pages 27 and 28
- 3 pieces of 2 1/2" x 2" white paper (6 x 5 cm)
- 1 silver button
- 2 paper fasteners
- stapler, scissors
- glue, felt pens
- X-acto® knife

Individual books:

The patterns on pages 27 and 28 can also be used to create individual books.

1

Place the bus template on the yellow tagboard. Trace around and cut out the shape. Cut a back cover and writing paper to match.

2

Use the wheel patterns to cut two wheels from the black squares. Attach them to the back cover with paper fasteners.

3

Draw students on white rectangles. Glue in place on the front cover. Glue on silver button "headlight."

4

Assemble the finished stories between the covers. Staple at the top. Fold and glue a strip of paper over the top edge and staples.

Literature Connections

Big Paul's School Bus by Paul Nichols; Prentice Hall, 1981.

Review school bus safety with Big Paul, the bus driver.

Bus Riders by Sharon Phillips Denslow; Four Winds Press, 1993.

Substitute bus drivers replace Lee, the regular driver.

The Magic School Bus Stories by Joanna Cole; Scholastic.

Go on exciting field trips with Miss Frizzle and her class in the Magic School Bus.

School Bus by Donald Crews; Puffin Books, 1985.

School buses take children to school and bring them home again.

The Wheels on the Bus by Maryann Kovalski; Little, Brown, 1987.

This is an illustrated version of the song of the same name.

Writing Connections

The Vanishing Yellow Bus

The bus disappears before your very eyes. What will you do now?

My Adventure on Bus 26

What happened to make the ride an adventure?

School Bus ABCs

I'm off to school and I'm taking a _____. Create an ABC book by changing the answer on each page—apple, book, coat, dictionary....

Empty —
Its riders wait,
Backpacks in place.
Then file on board
To find a space.

Full —
Passengers loaded.
Each seat occupied
The driver smiles,
"Let's go for a ride!"

Jill Norris

Something More to Do...

A Thank You for the Bus Driver

Prepare a surprise thank you for the bus driver.

1. Brainstorm with students to list all the duties and actions of a school bus driver. Choose the one duty that the students believe is most important. This will be reserved for page one and the final page.

2. Then assign each of the remaining duties to individual students. On separate pages illustrate and write about each duty or action.

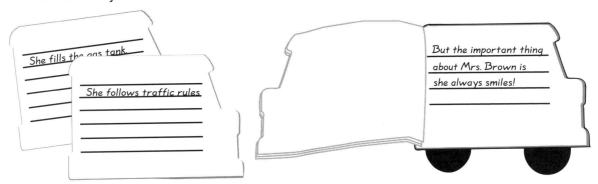

3. Put the book together as follows:

      First page: The important thing about Mrs. Brown is _____.
                          (this is where the most important duty goes—it might be she always smiles).
Pages in-between: She fills the gas tank.
                          She checks the tires.
                          She follows traffic rules.
                          She says good-bye.
      Last page: But the important thing about Mrs. Brown is (repeat the most important duty here).

Wheel Pattern

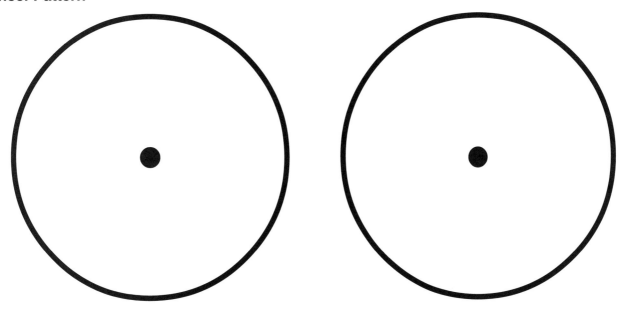

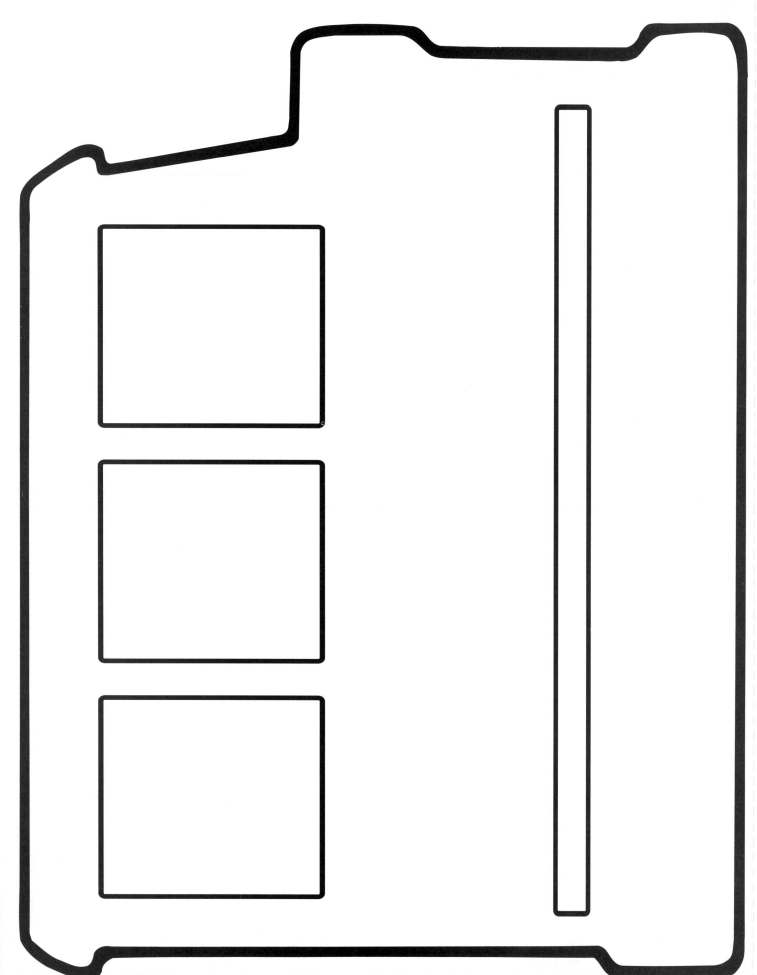

How to Make Books with Children EMC 777

The Lamb
A Shape Book

Materials

Class book:

- patterns on pages 31 and 32
- 1 sheet each of 9" x 12" (20 x 30.5 cm) black and white construction paper
- a 2" (5 cm) square of cardboard
- yarn
- two blue buttons; one red button
- hole punch, scissors
- glue, felt pens

Individual books:

The patterns on pages 31 and 32 can also be used to create individual books.

1

Cut out all of the pattern pieces.

2

Cut from black paper: lamb's body and legs (back cover), face, two ears.
Cut from white paper: lamb's body (front cover) top of lamb's head.
Cut writing paper in the shape of the body.

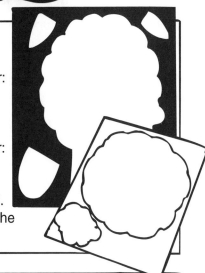

3

Assemble the head. Glue on buttons for eyes and nose. Glue the cardboard in the center of the white paper cover and glue the head on top.

4

Assemble all parts and punch two holes. Thread the yarn through the holes and tie in a bow.

Literature Connections

Borreguita and the Coyote by Verna Aardema; Scholastic, 1991.

A little lamb reasons with a coyote in this retelling of a Mexican tale.

The Lamb and the Butterfly by Arnold Sundgaard; Orchard Books, 1988.

A lamb and a butterfly discuss their different ways of life.

Sheep by Lynn M. Stone; Rouke Corporation Inc., 1990.

A nonfiction book filled with information and color photographs.

Smudge, the Little Lost Lamb by James Herrriot; St. Martin's Press, 1991.

Smudge finds a way under the fence and is soon lost.

Warm as Wool by Scott Russell Sanders; Bradbury Press, 1992.

A realistic story of a family of Ohio settlers who need warm clothing to survive the winter.

Writing Connections

My Warm Woolen_____

Write about and draw your favorite piece of woolen apparel.

Lost and Found

Little Bo-Peep has found her sheep. Tell where they were and how she got them home.

Strange Sheep

An unusual flock of sheep were discovered in the mountains.

Fluffy,
puffy,
fully,
woolly
sheep
Time to shear your wool.

Slimmer,
trimmer,
petite,
and neat
sheep
Now I have three bags full.

Jill Norris

Something More to Do...

Grazing Sheep

Create a picture of grazing sheep.

Materials:
- white paper
- paper plates
- cotton balls
- black marker
- tempera paints
  (green, black, white, blue)
- scissors

Steps to follow:

1. Paint green hills and a blue sky on your white paper. Let this background dry.

2. Squeeze puddles of black and white paint onto separate paper plates.

3. Dip the cotton balls into a puddle of paint. Print on the green pasture. (To print, push the cotton ball straight down and pull it straight up. Don't draw with the cotton ball.) One print = one sheep.

4. Make a fingerprint with black paint for the head of each sheep.

5. After the paint is dry, use a marker to draw legs and ears. Let your sheep point in different directions. Have some sheep eating grass while others look at each other or at the sky.

6. Add some fluffy clouds by printing with a cotton ball dipped in white paint.

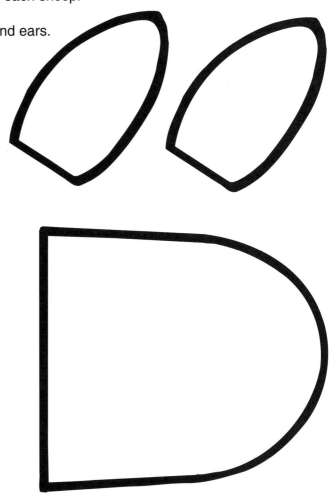

How to Make Books with Children EMC 777

How to Make Books with Children EMC 777

The Shoe
A Shape Book

Materials

Class book:

- shoe pattern on page 36
- 2 sheets of 9" x 12" (20 x 30.5 cm) construction paper or tagboard
- a brightly-colored shoe lace
- student writing paper
- hole punch, scissors
- glue, felt pens

Individual book:

Reproduce the pattern on page 36 for each student to color, cut, and use as a cover for an original story. Use roving or yarn to lace the book.

1

Color and cut out the pattern.

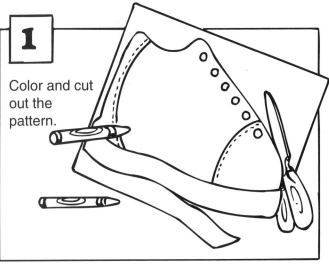

2

Glue the pattern to the construction paper. Cut around the shape leaving a small border. This is the front cover.

Cut the back cover and student writing papers in the same shape.

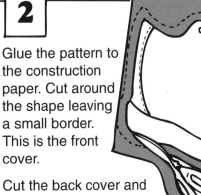

3

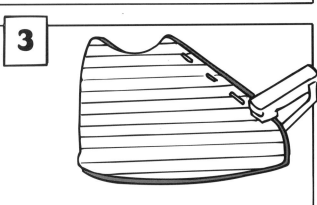

Staple the writing papers to the back cover.

4

Assemble all layers. Punch holes along the top.

Lace the shoelace through the holes.

33

Literature Connections

The Bat in the Boot by Annie Cannon; Orchard Books, 1996.

A baby bat is found in a boot and rescued.

Benjamin Bigfoot by Mary Serfozo; Margaret K. McElderry Books, 1993.

When Benjamin wears his dad's old shoes he feels grown-up, so he wants to wear them to kindergarten.

Big Shoe, Little Shoe by Denys Cazet; Bradbury Press, 1984.

Grandpa and little Louie change jobs and shoes throughout the day.

Bird's New Shoes by Chris Riddell; Henry Holt & Company, 1987.

The animals of the forest argue about the latest fashions in clothing.

Feet by Peter Parnall; Macmillan, 1988.

In simple words and pictures, this book describes different feet.

Mrs. Toggle's Beautiful Blue Shoe by Robin Pulver; Four Winds Press, 1994.

When Mrs. Toggle joins her class in a game of kickball, her shoe ends up in a tree.

My Best Shoes by Marilee Robin Burton; Tambourine Books, 1994.

The rhyming text celebrates the variety of shoes worn on different days of the week.

My Two Shoes by Alice Schertle; Lothrop, Lee & Shepard, 1985.

A young girl describes the adventures she had, year-round, with her two feet.

Shoes by Elizabeth Winthrop; Harper & Row, 1986.

A survey of many kinds of shoes concludes that the best "shoes" are bare feet.

Writing Connections

Don't Walk Through That Mud!

Write a story from a sneaker's point of view.

Magic Sneakers

Where did you find them? What can they do for you? What happened when you wore them?

How Sneakers Got Their Name

Write a story to tell how you think sneakers earned their name.

Tiny booties on baby feet,
Workmen's boots walking
        down the street,
Dainty slippers, high tops for
        running,
Flip flops and sandals — good
        for sunning:
Shoes of every shape and size
Help your feet to specialize.

Jill Norris

Something More to Do...

Careful Descriptions

Practice describing things accurately by creating a shoe riddle book, **Whose Shoes?**

1. Brainstorm ways to describe a shoe—its color, size, shape, purpose, age, condition... Record these suggestions as headings on a chart. Then add adjectives to the chart—brown, enormous, high-topped, work-boot, old, scuffed—forming a word bank.

My Shoe

Color	Size	Material	Condition
Black	1	Patent Leather	Shiny, new
Blue	4	Canvas	Old, worn, frayed laces
White	6	Leather and Fabric	Clean

2. Have students take off one of their shoes and look at it carefully. Challenge them to describe their own shoes using the chart categories. Write a riddle describing the shoe.

> I'm white and flexible. I'm happiest when I'm on the court playing a certain kind of sport. Six months is about as long as I'm good. I have a "tongue" and lots of "eyes." What am I?

3. Copy final shoe riddles onto individual pages for a class book. Add an illustration or a photograph of the shoe on each page and ask **"Whose Shoe?"** Write riddle answers on the backs of pages.

4. Share the riddles as a guessing game.

Note: Ask parents to create a similar book at Parents' Night.
Students will love guessing which shoes belong to their parents.

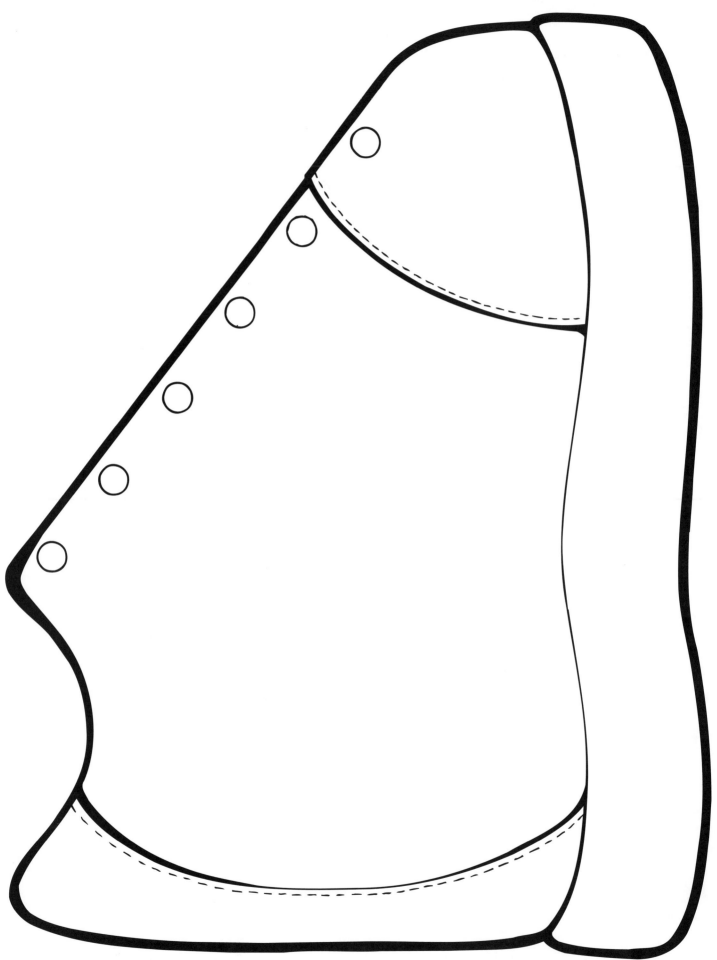

36

How to Make Books with Children EMC 777

The Egg
A Pop-up Book

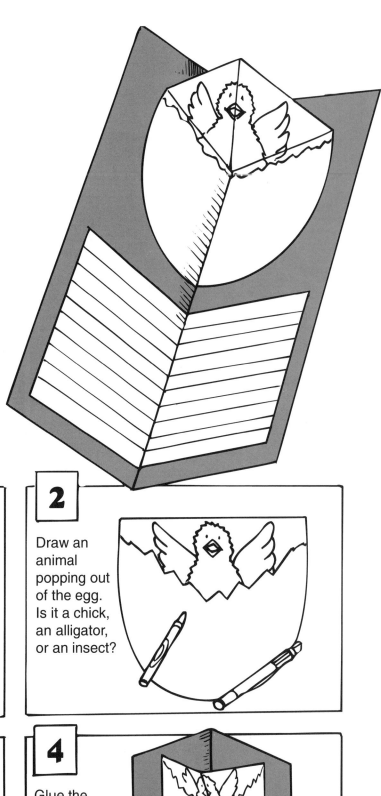

Materials

Individual books:

- front cover form on page 39
- pop-up form on page 40
- 12" x 18" (30.5 x 45.5 cm) construction paper
- writing paper
- crayons or felt pens
- glue, scissors

Class book:

See binding instructions on page 3.

1

Cut out the pop-up form and follow the folding directions shown here.

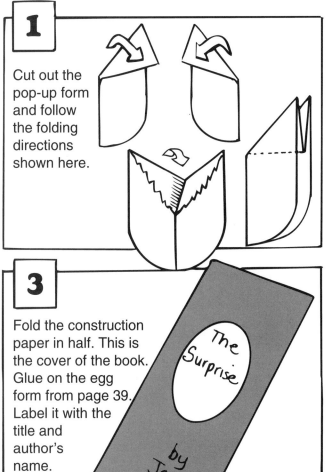

2

Draw an animal popping out of the egg. Is it a chick, an alligator, or an insect?

3

Fold the construction paper in half. This is the cover of the book. Glue on the egg form from page 39. Label it with the title and author's name.

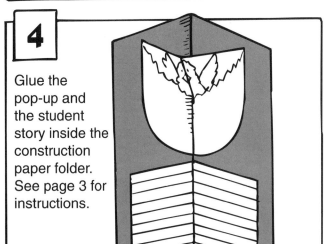

The Surprise
by Joy

4

Glue the pop-up and the student story inside the construction paper folder. See page 3 for instructions.

How to Make Books with Children EMC 777

Literature Connections

Chickens Aren't the Only Ones by Ruth Heller; Grosset & Dunlop, 1981.

Rhyming text describes many oviparous creatures.

Egg! by A. J. Wood; Little, Brown, 1993.

The reader unfolds the pages to discover what kind of creatures hatch out of twelve different eggs.

Egg—A Photographic Story of Hatching by Robert Burton; Dorling Kindersley, 1994.

Photographs show many different eggs and chronicle changes as they hatch.

Hatch, Egg, Hatch by Shen Roddie and Frances Cony; Little, Brown, 1991.

Mother Hen tries to get her egg to hatch.

Just Plain Fancy by Patricia Polacco; Bantam Books, 1990.

An Amish girl finds a "fancy" egg and puts it in the hen's nest to hatch.

The Most Wonderful Egg in the World by Helme Heine; Atheneum, 1983.

A king tried to judge which hen lays the most beautiful egg.

Rechenka's Eggs by Patricia Polacco; Philomel Books, 1988.

When Babuska rescues an injured goose, it returns the favor and lays thirteen special eggs.

Writing Connections

The Fantastic Egg

Describe the most fantastic egg that you can imagine. What do you think will hatch from it?

The Egg That Wouldn't Crack

Mother Bird had a nest full of eggs. When all but one hatch, Mother Bird looks for a way to crack the stubborn egg. Write about what she does.

Eggcellent!!

Create a recipe for a new dish using eggs as one of the ingredients.

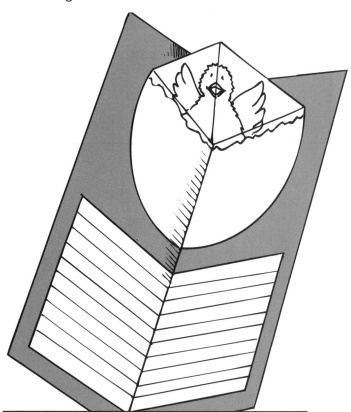

**A place of beginnings
That's easy to break,
It might hold a spider,
A chick, or a snake.**

Jill Norris

Something More to Do...

Oviparous Creatures

Materials:
- construction paper
  - 6" x 12" (15 x 30.5 cm) paper in pink, blue, or spring green
  - 1" x 4" (2.5 x 10 cm) strip for "spring"
  - small scraps
- a copy of egg pattern below
- scissors, glue
- felt pens or crayons

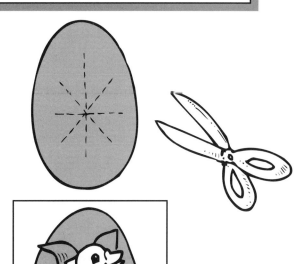

Steps to follow:
1. Make an egg.
   - Cut out egg shape. Decorate the shape with crayon or felt pens.
   - Cut a starburst pattern on the egg as shown. Pull back each section. Press down or curl on a pencil.
   - Glue the egg to a background sheet.

2. Make a creature.
   - Create a tiny animal from construction paper scraps.
   - Glue it to an accordion pleated "spring."
   - Glue the other end of the spring inside the opening in the egg. The little animal will peek out of the cracked egg.

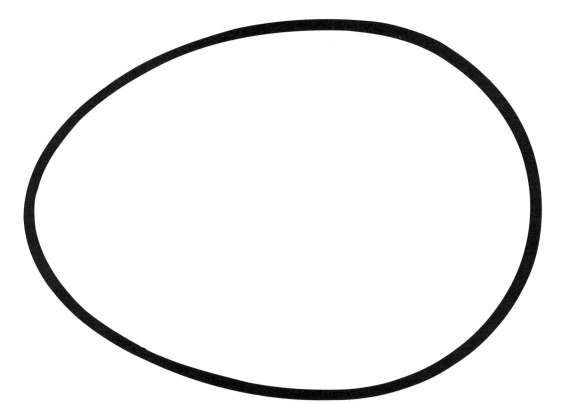

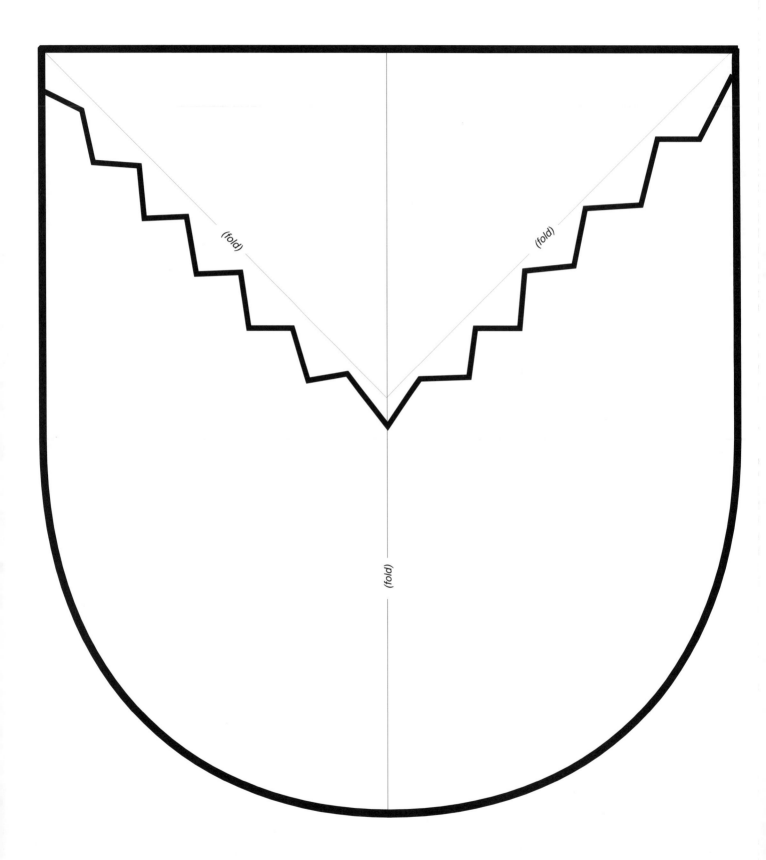

(fold)

(fold)

(fold)

My Shadow
A Pop-Up Book

Materials

Class book:

- pop-up forms and patterns on pages 43–44
- 12" x 18" (30.5 x 45.5 cm) blue construction paper
- black construction paper
- writing paper
- scissors, glue
- felt pens or crayons
- stapler

1 Cut and fold the pop-up pattern on page 44.

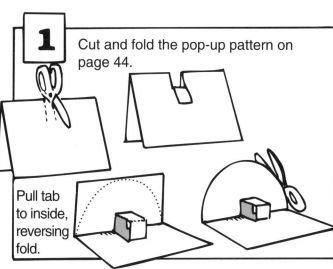

Pull tab to inside, reversing fold.

2 Cut out the person pattern on page 43. Cut the same pattern out of black paper.

Add features and clothing to the person and glue to the pop-up tab.

Glue the shadow on the "ground."

3 Measure 5 1/2" down the sides of the construction paper and fold.

Glue the pop-up on the fold. See page 3 for instructions. Cut around the pattern.

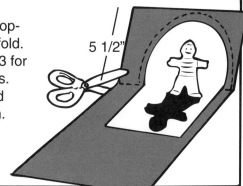

5 1/2"

4 Glue the sun behind the pop-up.

Glue the writing paper below the pop-up.

Assemble stories and bind with a front and back cover.

How to Make Books with Children EMC 777

Literature Connections

Bear Shadow by Frank Asch; Prentice Hall, 1985.

Bear tries to get rid of his shadow.

The Boy with Two Shadows by Margaret Maky; J. B. Lippincott, 1987.

Two shadows can be a problem.

Footprints and Shadows by Anne Wescott Dodd; Simon & Schuster, 1992.

Where do shadows go when the snow melts? What happens to shadows when the light changes?

My Shadow by Robert Louis Stevenson; G. P. Putnam's Sons, 1990.

An illustrated version of Robert Louis Stevenson's famous poem.

Nothing Sticks Like a Shadow by Ann Tompert; Houghton Mifflin, 1984.

Rabbit tries to get rid of his shadow.

Writing Connections

Hiding from My Shadow

Where would you hide from your shadow? Write about what happens when you try to carry out your plan.

Games to Play with Your Shadow

Make up some games that you could play with your shadow. Name the games, and write the rules for playing.

My Thoughts, by Your Shadow

What would your shadow say if it could talk? Look at the things you do from your shadow's point of view.

When the shining sun comes up
My shadow comes to play.
It stays to run around with me
Until it is midday.

Then in the afternoon
It saunters back in sight,
To stay until the sun leaves
When daytime turns to night.

Jill Norris

Something More to Do...

Seeing Shadows

1. Tape a large piece of newsprint on the wall. Set up a projector on a low table so that its light shines on the paper. Allow enough space between the projector and the wall for students to move. Let every student have a chance to make shadows in front of the light. (Warn students that looking straight at the light can hurt their eyes.)

2. Discuss the prerequisites for a shadow — a light source and something that blocks the light. Use simple shadow puppets made by drawing shapes on stiff paper, cutting them out, and taping them to craft sticks. Have students sit in front of the projector holding their stick puppets and facing the newsprint on the wall. Turn on the projector light and have students hold their puppets so that they make shadows on the wall.
   - How can the shadow's size be changed?
   - How can the shadow's shape be changed?

3. Go outside on a dry, sunny morning. Find a large concrete area and mark it off as a "Do Not Enter" zone for the day. Choose one person to be the shadow model. Use chalk to draw around the model's feet. Then draw around the model's shadow. Note the time and measure the shadow, recording its height. (Write the time and the measurements on the shadow.) Three or four more times during the day, return to the same spot to measure the shadow again. Have the model stand in the traced footprints, trace the shadow, and measure it.
   - How has the shadow changed?
   - What caused the change?

Figure and Shadow Pattern

         How to Make Books with Children EMC 777

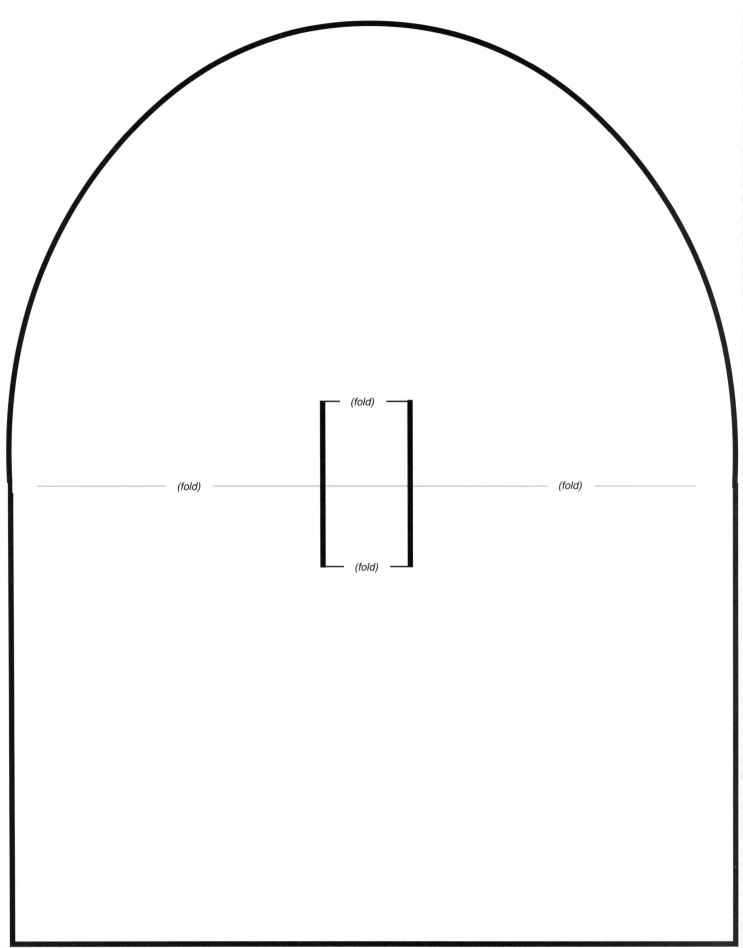

(fold)

(fold)   (fold)

(fold)

 How to Make Books with Children EMC 777

The Frog
A Pop-Up Book

Materials

Individual books:

- pop-up form on page 48
- frog feet pattern on page 47
- 2 sheets of 9" x 12" (20 x 30.5 cm) blue paper
- writing paper
- a 1 1/2" x 9" (cm) strip of blue paper
- scissors, glue
- felt pens or crayons

1

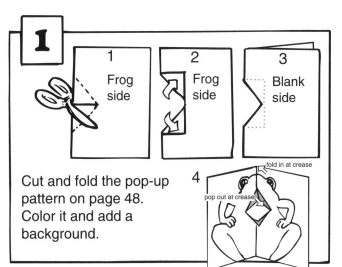

1 Frog side

2 Frog side

3 Blank side

4 fold in at crease / pop out at crease

Cut and fold the pop-up pattern on page 48. Color it and add a background.

2 Fold both pieces of blue paper.

Glue the pop-up inside the first folder. (See page 3 for instructions.)

Color and cut out the frog feet. Glue them to the pattern.

3 Glue a writing paper inside the second folder.

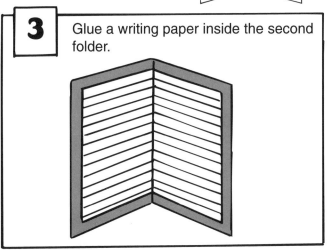

4 Lay the two sheets of paper side by side. Glue the paper strip down the center. Fold.

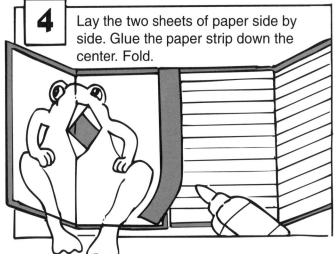

How to Make Books with Children EMC 777

Literature Connections

Frog Medicine by Mark Teague; Scholastic, 1991.

Elmo discovers that putting off an assignment is not a good idea.

The Frog Prince Continues by Jon Scieszka; Viking Penguin, 1992.

This is a story about what happened after the Princess kissed the frog and changed him into a Prince.

Little Frog's Song by Alice Schertle; HarperCollins, 1992.

A little frog is washed away from his pond during a storm.

Moon, Stars, Frogs, and Friends by Patricia MacLachlan, 1980.

Randall, the frog, is looking for a real friend.

Tuesday by David Wiesner; Clarion Books, 1991.

This Caldecott winner is almost wordless. It tells a story about the bewitching hour on Tuesday when frogs can fly.

The Wide-Mouthed Frog by Rex Schneider; Stemmer House, 1980.

A frog asks the advice of other swamp animals on proper diet; then he meets an alligator.

Writing Connections

Party on a Lilypad

Describe a frog birthday party. How would it be different than a human party?

The Hungry Frog

List special treats for a frog to eat. Try listing at least one for each letter of the alphabet.
> amazing aphid...
> buzzing bee...
> crawling cicada...
> dancing dragonfly...

Frog Secrets

Frog has a secret and he's not telling anybody. What could it be?

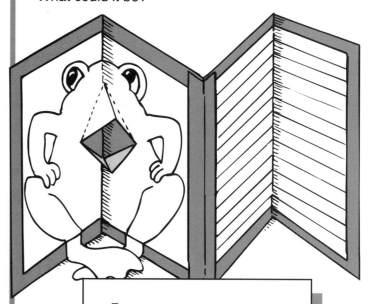

**Long tongue,
Big eyes,
Loud croak,
Eats flies,
High jumps,
Webbed feet,
Proud pond
Athlete.**

Jill Norris

Something More to Do...

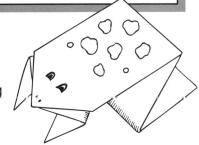

Jumping Frogs

Materials:
- rectangles of lightweight paper — 3" x 5 1/2" (7.5 x 14 cm) for a small frog
  6" x 11" (15 x 28 cm) for a larger frog

Note: Plain copy paper works well. Wrapping paper makes special frogs.

Steps to follow:
1. Fold the paper.

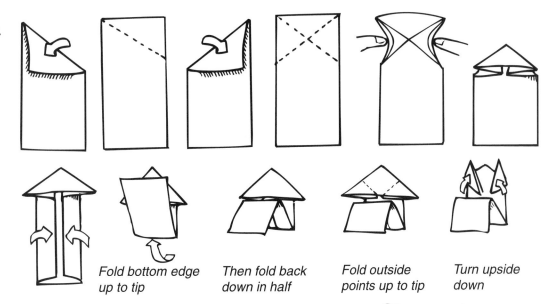

Fold bottom edge up to tip

Then fold back down in half

Fold outside points up to tip

Turn upside down

2. Color eyes and add details.

3. Make the frog jump by stroking the frog's back gently.

Extensions:
- After reading *Tuesday,* mount the frogs on lily pads and hang them from the ceiling.
- Write about where you would fly if you were a frog on that special Tuesday.

Patterns for Frog Feet

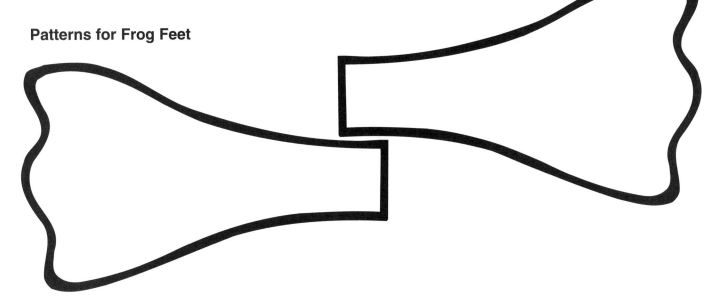

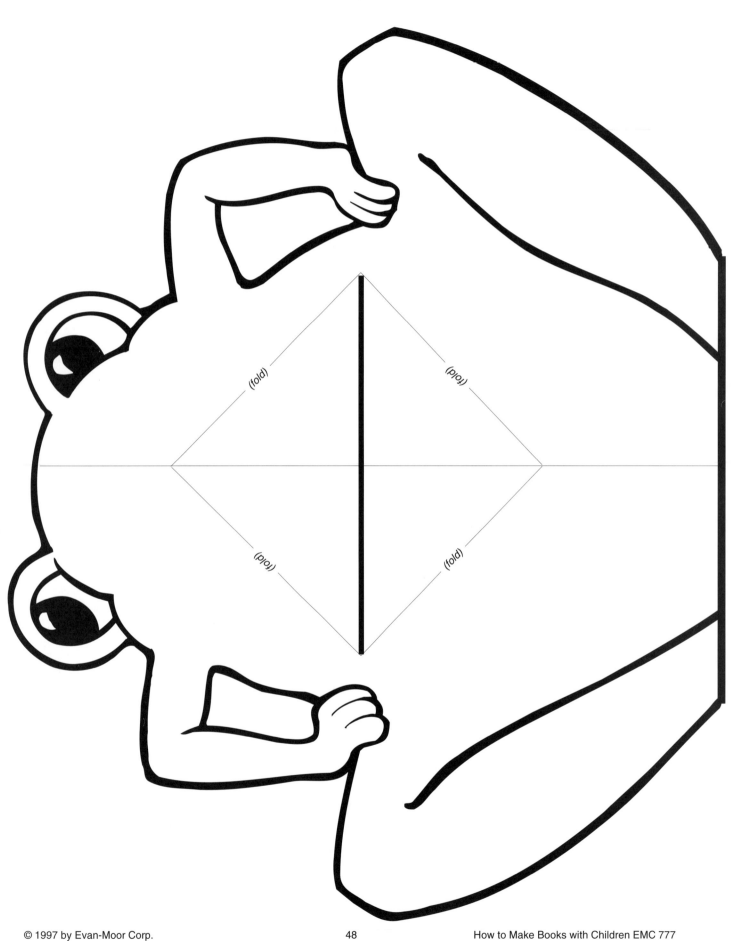

(fold)

(fold)

(fold)

(fold)

How to Make Books with Children EMC 777

The Purse
A Pop-Up Book

Materials

Individual books:

- purse pattern on page 52
- pop-up pattern on page 51
- 12" x 18" (30.5 x 45.5 cm) sheet of construction paper
- paper scraps
- yarn or ribbon
- scissors, hole punch
- felt pens or crayons

1 Fold the construction paper in half.

Color and cut out the purse pattern. Glue it to the outside of the folder.

Cut around the purse pattern, leaving a border of colored paper.

2 Cut and fold the pop-up form. Have students write their story on the lines.

Pull tabs to inside, reversing fold.

3 Glue the pop-up form in the fold of the construction paper. (See pop-up tips, page 3.)

Use scrap paper to create the objects that are to be in the purse. Glue them on the pop-up form.

4 Tie a single strip in the outside holes to use as a handle.

Punch three holes across the top. Tie a yarn strip in each of the center holes. These strips tie together to close the purse.

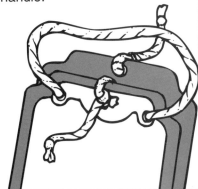

Literature Connections

The Lady with the Alligator Purse **by Nadine Bernard Westcott; Little, Brown, 1988.**

Read this illustrated version of the traditional song.

The Magic Purse **retold by Yoshiko Uchida; Margaret K. McElderry Books, 1993.**

A poor farmer escapes two dangerous swamps with a magic purse.

The Purse **by Kathy Caple; Houghton Mifflin, 1986.**

Katie spends her money to buy a purse and now must figure out how to get more money to put in it.

Writing Connections

The Lost Purse

Mother went shopping and lost her purse. Tell what happened. Was the purse found?

The Purse of the Future

What will the purse of the future look like? Will it have a mini-computer? A button to push to unlock your front door? A built-in umbrella? Write about your ideas.

The Magic Purse

Write your own version of a story about a magic purse. What special powers will your purse have? Who will own the purse?

Something More to Do...

ABC Purse

Use a large purse as a prop to reinforce letter-sound associations.

- Label the purse with a specific letter. Fill the purse with a variety of objects. Students will remove those objects that don't begin with the sound the letter stands for.

- As you study a letter, put an object representing that letter into the purse. Review the letters you have studied by removing the items from the purse and matching them with letter cards.

Design a Purse

Your favorite story character may need a special purse. Challenge your students to design one.

For example:
Cinderella's purse might include an alarm clock to remind her of the midnight curfew, some scouring pads for quick clean-up jobs, a spare pair of shoes in case she loses one, and an I.D. so that she can identify herself.

> **My grandma has a big black purse**
> **With zippers and pockets galore.**
> **Just reach inside and you will find**
> **Anything you'd buy at a store!**
>
> *Jill Norris*

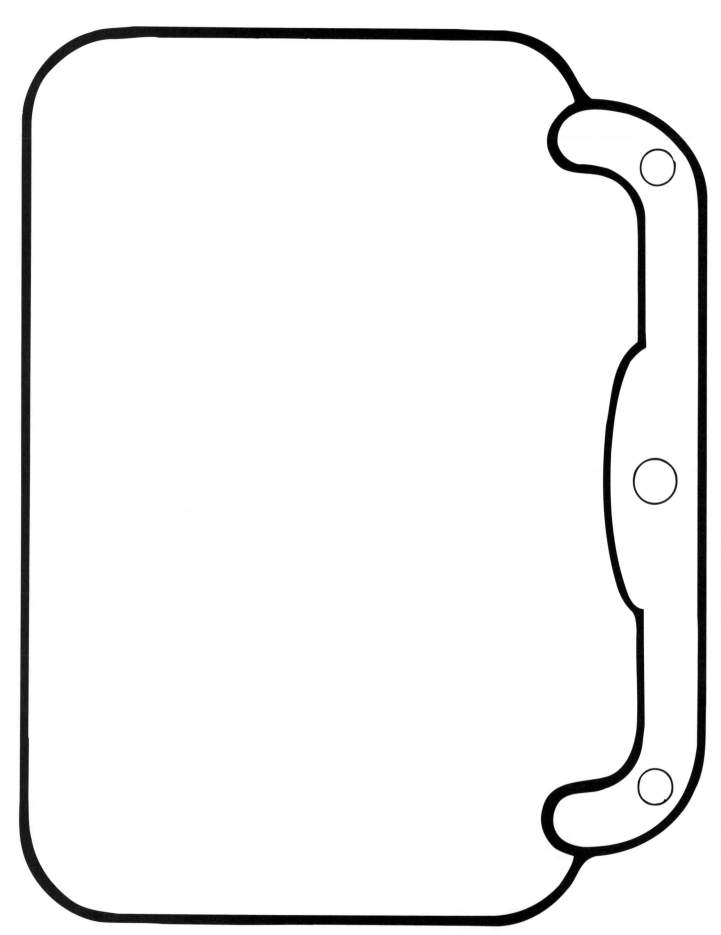

52

The Dragon
A Pop-Up Book

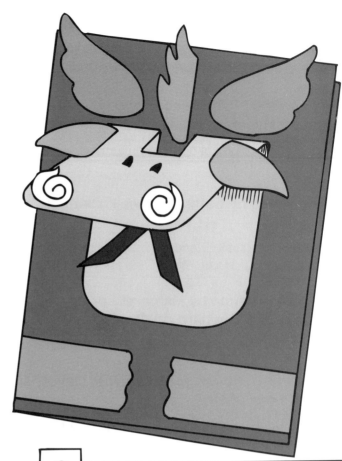

Materials

Individual books:

- 1 copy of the patterns on page 56
- 2 copies of the patterns on page 55
- 12" x 18" (30.5 x 45.5 cm) sheet of green construction paper
- writing paper
- paper scraps
- glue, scissors
- felt pens, crayons
- stapler

1 Cut and fold the pop-up pattern for the dragon's head.

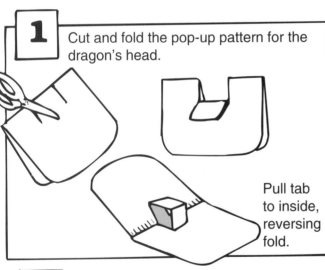

Pull tab to inside, reversing fold.

2 Glue the back side of the dragon's head to the front of the green folder, 4" from the top.

Glue the flames inside the mouth.

3 Cut out the remaining patterns. Color them and glue to the book cover.

scales
wings
ears
nostrils
paws

4 Glue or staple the story paper inside the folder.

53

Literature Connections

Anna and the Little Green Dragon **by Klaus Baungart; Hyperion Books, 1992.**

Anna opens her box of corn flakes and out comes a little green dragon.

Dragon Tooth **by Cathryn Falwell; Clarion Books, 1996.**

Sara has a loose tooth and is afraid to pull it until she creates a cardboard dragon and pulls its tooth.

Eyes of the Dragon **by Margaret Leaf; Lothrop, Lee & Shepard, 1987.**

The painting of a dragon on a wall comes to life.

Herbert the Timid Dragon **by Mercer Mayer; Golden Press, 1980.**

A timid dragon, who dreams of being a knight, tries to rescue a princess.

Jack and the Fire Dragon **by Gail E. Haley; Crown Publishers, 1988.**

An Appalachian tale about the time that Jack rescued three beautiful sisters from the Fire Dragon.

St. George and the Dragon **retold by Margaret Hodges; Little, Brown, 1984.**

This Caldecott winner has amazing illustrations, a brave knight, and a beautiful princess.

The Loathsome Dragon **retold by David Wiesner and Kim Kahng; G. P. Putnam's Sons, 1987.**

A wicked queen casts a spell over her beautiful stepdaughter turning her into a fierce dragon.

There's A Dragon About **by Richard and Roni Schotter; Orchard Books, 1994.**

A rhyming report of a winter revel performance with suggestions for putting on your own entertainment.

Writing Connections

Getting Rid of Dragons

You are a brave knight of the Round Table and you have just been assigned the job of ridding the kingdom of all its dragons. What plans will you make? How will you carry them out?

Baby Dragon

A baby dragon has just hatched from an egg that you found. Describe the baby and tell what you will do to care for it.

Dragon Power

Knights and kings are always killing dragons. What solution do you have to put dragons to productive use? Write about positive ways to use dragon-power.

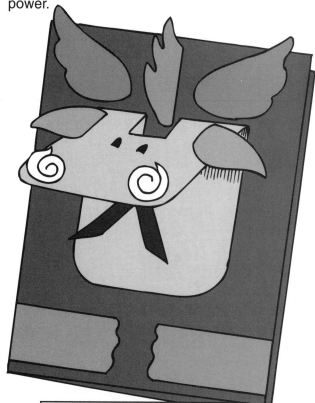

Fiery breath,
Flashing eye,
Dragon soars
Across the sky.

Jill Norris

Something More to Do...

Cooperative Dragons

Encourage cooperative work by assigning a group dragon project.

1. After reading several stories with good dragon descriptions, divide your class into groups of 4-5. Ask each group to create a dragon.

2. Individual group members are responsible for specific parts, but must communicate with the group in order to create a unified whole. After discussion, groups should assign one dragon part to each group member (head, body, legs, tail, wings).

3. Provide large paper, paint, crayons, markers, colored paper scraps, newspaper, tissue paper, aluminum foil, scissors, glue, staplers, and other available art supplies. Set a time limit and stand back.

   Note: You may need to act as a negotiator. Encourage teams to solve their own problems.

Dragon Parts Patterns

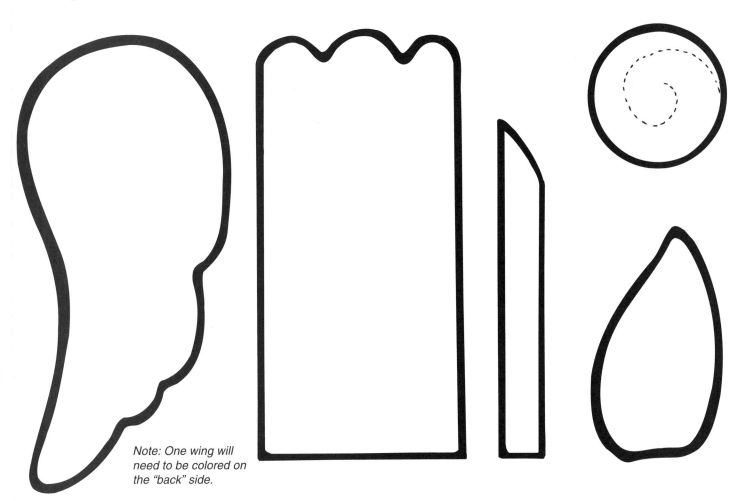

Note: One wing will need to be colored on the "back" side.

         How to Make Books with Children EMC 777

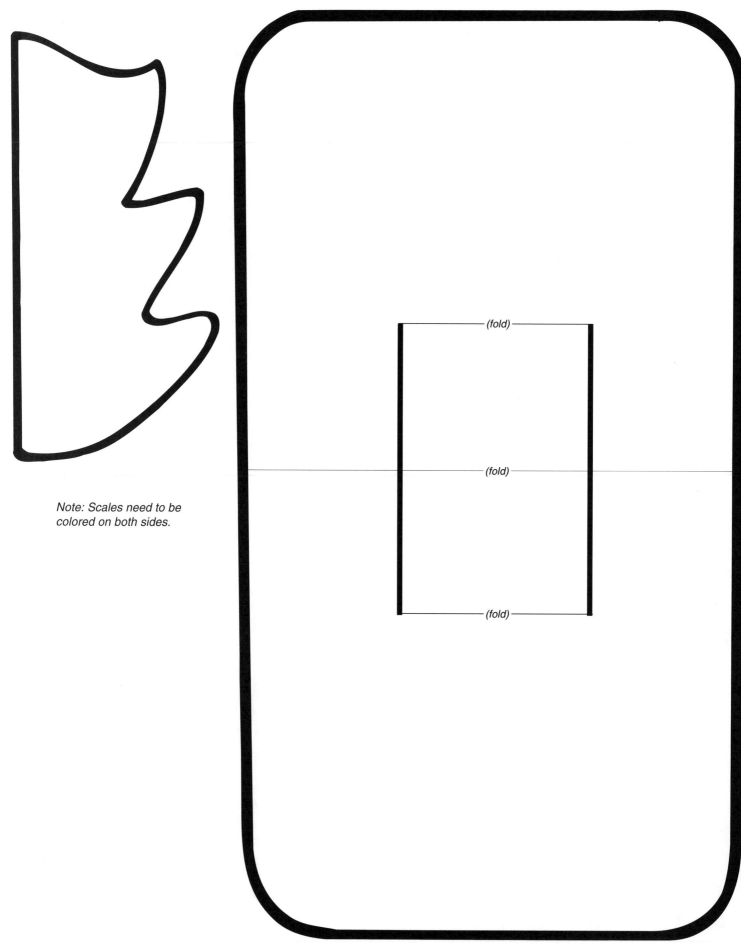

Note: Scales need to be colored on both sides.

(fold)

(fold)

(fold)

How to Make Books with Children EMC 777

Red Riding Hood

A Pop-Up Book

Individual books:

- Red Riding Hood pattern on page 59
- pop-up wolf pattern on page 60
- 12" x 18" (30.5 x 45.5 cm) construction paper
- paper scraps
- writing paper
- scissors, glue
- felt pens or crayons

1

Color, cut, and fold the pop-up pattern.

2 Fold the construction paper in half.

Glue the pop-up in the center fold. (See pop-up binding on page 3.)

Glue the writing paper below the pop-up.

3

Make a small Red Riding Hood to glue inside wolf's mouth using the pattern on page 59.

4

Put a title and the author's name on the front cover.

Little Red Riding Hood

by Sam

How to Make Books with Children EMC 777

Literature Connections

Here are six versions of the well-known tale of a little girl who takes a basket of goodies to her grandmother.

Flossie & the Fox by Patricia C. McKissack; Dial Books, 1986.

LIttle Red Riding Hood retold by Trina Schart Hyman; Holiday House, 1983.

Little Red Riding Hood: A New Fangled Prairie Tale by Lisa Campbell Ernst; Simon & Schuster, 1995.

Red Riding Hood retold by James Marshall; Dial Books, 1987.

Red Riding Hood by Christopher Coady; Dutton Children's Books, 1991.

Ruby's Storm by Amy Hest; Four Winds Press, 1994.

On a stormy day, Ruby travels across the city to visit her grandfather.

Writing Connections

A Basket of Goodies

What would you put in a goodie basket and who would you give it to? Use the answers to these questions as the basis of a story.

Lost in the Woods

Write an adventure about someone lost in the woods.

The Wolf's Story

Tell the story of Red Riding Hood from the wolf's point of view.

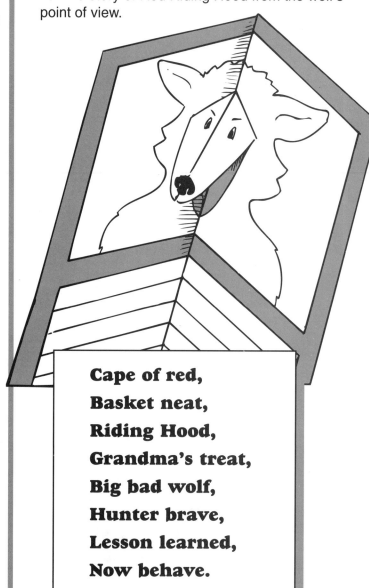

Cape of red,
Basket neat,
Riding Hood,
Grandma's treat,
Big bad wolf,
Hunter brave,
Lesson learned,
Now behave.

Jill Norris

Something More to Do...

A New Red Riding Hood

1. After reading several versions of the traditional tale of Red Riding Hood, identify elements that are common to every story. List the items on a chart.

2. Challenge students to write yet another version of the tale. Change the elements in some way.
   • What if the wolf were a spider?
   • What if Red Riding Hood wore a denim jacket and a baseball hat?
   • What if Red Riding Hood were male?

3. Share your stories and enjoy the creativity.

> ### Red Riding Hood
> 1. girl going to visit her grandmother
>
> 2. wolf who is up to no good
>
> 3. sick grandmother

Red Riding Hood Pattern

How to Make Books with Children EMC 777

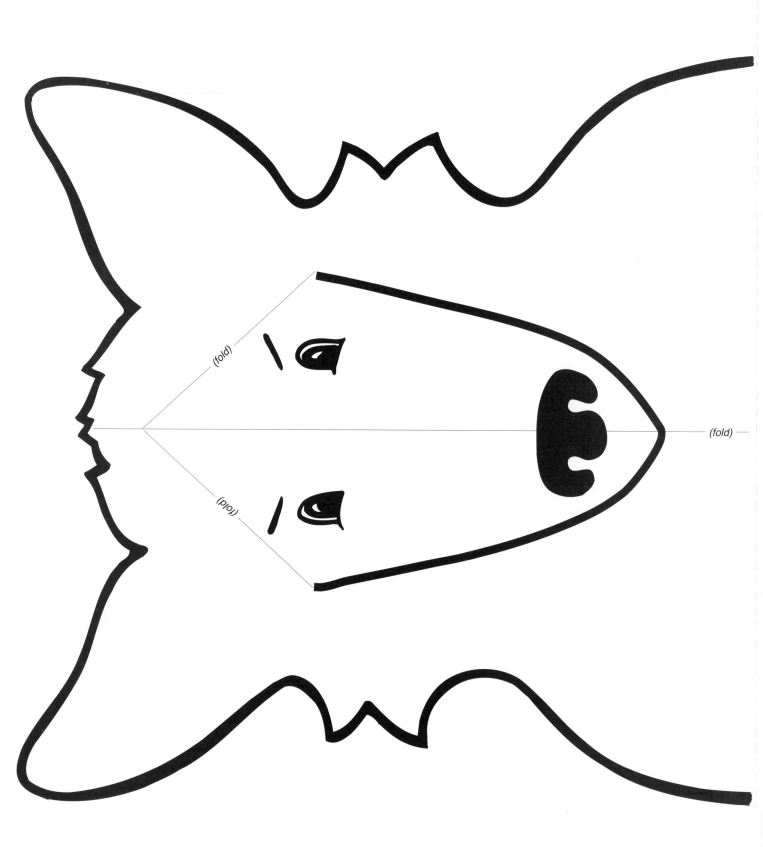

(fold)

(fold)

(fold)

Lunch Box

A Pop-Up Book

1 Fold and cut the pop-up form.

Pull tabs to inside, reversing fold.

2 Fold the construction paper. Round the corners of the folder.

Glue the pop-up in the construction paper folder.

3

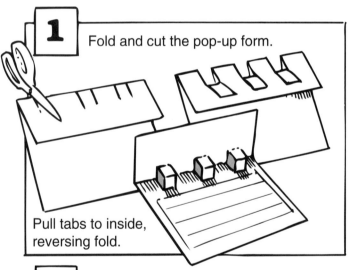

Cut out food items from the construction paper pieces. Glue them to the pop-up tabs.

4 Decorate the cover sheet with a title and picture.

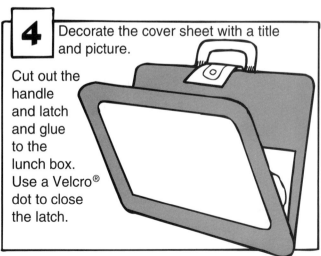

Cut out the handle and latch and glue to the lunch box. Use a Velcro® dot to close the latch.

Literature Connections

***Grandpa's Garden Lunch* by Judith Caselye; Greenwillow, 1990.**

Sarah and her grandparents enjoy a lunch made from homegrown vegetables.

***The Green Hornet Lunchbox* by Shirley Gordan; Houghton Mifflin, 1970.**

Joey gets a new lunch box and then he finds out that his best friend eats school lunches.

***Halmoni and the Picnic* by Sook Nyul Choi; Houghton Mifflin, 1993.**

When her Korean grandma is lonely, Yunmi decides to help her feel at home in America.

***I Need a Lunch Box* by Jeannette Caines; Harper & Row, 1988.**

A little boy wants a lunch box.

***Lunch* by Denise Fleming; Henry Holt & Company, 1992.**

A very hungry mouse eats a huge lunch.

***Lunch Boxes* by Fred Ehrlich; Puffin Books, 1991.**

Lunchtime at Oak Street School is a noisy, messy affair.

Writing Connections

You'll Never Guess What I Found!

When I opened my lunch box today I found a...

The Perfect Lunch for_____

Choose an interesting person and tell what you would pack in his/her lunch box. You might choose a football player, Batman, an astronaut, the President...

Never Carry _____ in Your Lunchbox

Tell why you shouldn't carry a particular item in your lunch box.

> **I can't wait to open it.**
> **What will be inside?**
> **Maybe it's some yogurt**
> **Or a piece of chicken, fried.**
> **Maybe it's a sandwich —**
> **Turkey or P. B. and J.**
> **I wonder what's inside**
> **My <u>new</u> lunch box today.**
>
> *Jill Norris*

Something More to Do...

Lunch Box Databank

Help students to practice analysis with the contents of their lunch boxes.

1. Have students list the contents of their lunch boxes.

    1 roast beef sandwich, carrot sticks, two cookies, a banana, milk

2. Create a master list of all lunch box ingredients. Group the items on the master list in the four basic food groups — grains and breads, fruits and vegetables, milk products, and meat and poultry.

3. Have students make tally marks beside items that were in their lunches.

4. Analyze the tally by asking questions such as:

    • Which item on the master list was in the most lunch boxes?
    • Which items were least popular?
    • Which food group was included most often?

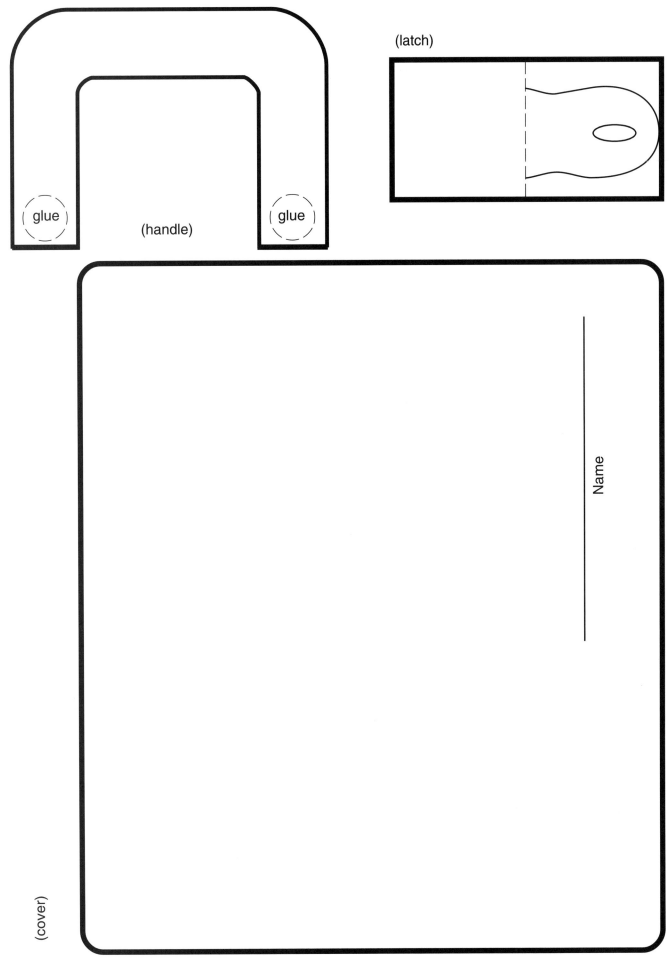

(latch)

glue   (handle)   glue

(cover)

Name

How to Make Books with Children EMC 777

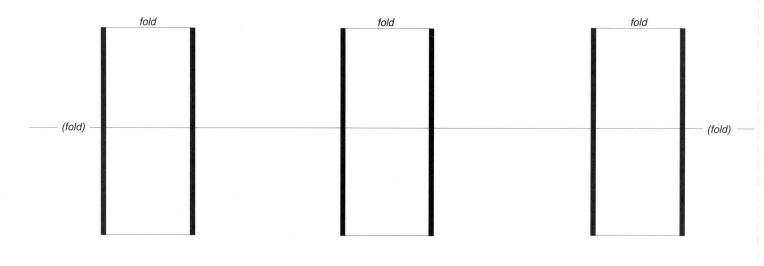

fold

fold

fold

(fold)

(fold)

The Dog
A Pop-Up Book

Materials

Class or individual book:

- pop-up patterns on pages 67–68
- 12" x 18" (30.5 x 45.5 cm) construction paper
- 12" x 13" (30.5 x 43.3 cm) construction paper cover sheet
- writing paper
- felt pens or crayons
- scissors, glue

1 Fold 5" (13 cm) in on the construction paper.

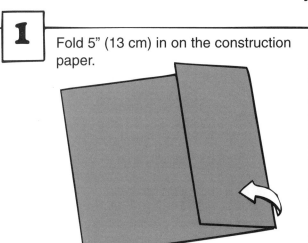

2 Color and cut out the patterns. Follow the folding directions for the pop-up.

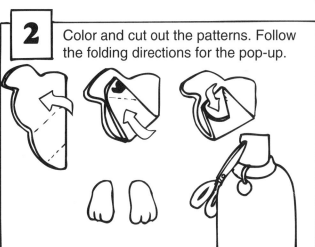

3 Glue the patterns in the folded area of the construction paper.

4 Glue student stories next to the pop-up.

Staple all the stories together with a front cover.

Cover the staples by gluing a paper strip over the edge.

How to Make Books with Children · 777

Literature Connections

Dogs Don't Wear Sneakers **by Laura Numeroff; Simon & Schuster, 1993.**

A book of animal rhymes that encourages the imagination.

The Dog Who Had Kittens **by Polly Robertus; The Trumpet Club, 1988.**

A heartwarming tale of a basset hound who helps to raise a litter of kittens.

Raining Cats and Dogs **by Jane Yolen; Harcourt Brace & Company, 1993.**

A book of poems about cats and dogs.

Wag Wag Wag **by Peter Hansard; Candlewick Press, 1993.**

Single words describe the activities of a variety of dogs.

Where's Spot? **and other *Spot* books by Eric Hill; G. P. Putnam's Sons.**

Lift the flap and read about the adventures of the puppy named Spot and his friends.

Writing Connections

Teaching a Dog a Trick

Imagine that your teacher believed that students should be taught in the same way as dogs. Describe how he/she would teach the class to do a math problem. Be sure to include proper rewards.

Can He Talk?

Write a story telling what you think your pet dog would say to you if he/she could talk.

The Best Dog in the World

Tell about what the best dog in the world would be like.

> **The puppies pounce.**
> **The puppies race.**
> **They dash about**
> **At a breakneck pace.**
>
> **The puppies wrestle.**
> **The puppies sleep**
> **Piled on their cushion**
> **In a doggie heap.**
>
> *Jill Norris*

Something More to Do...

Identifying Synonyms — Different Ways to Say the Same Thing

Create a chart by following these steps:
1. Discuss with your class the many different words that are used to name a dog: pup, hound, pooch... List these words on the chart.
2. Now, choose a describing word like *running* and list all of the different synonyms for it.
3. Choose a place word like *home* and list all of the different synonyms for it.

Have students write sentences using one word from each list. Although each sentence means essentially the same thing, the connotations of the sentence can be quite different. Now is a good time to discuss the idea of connotation with your class.
- Share the sentences that they have written.
- Discuss how word choice affects the picture that the sentence makes in the reader's mind.
- Use the sentence as part of a short story. Observe how the word choice affected the story.

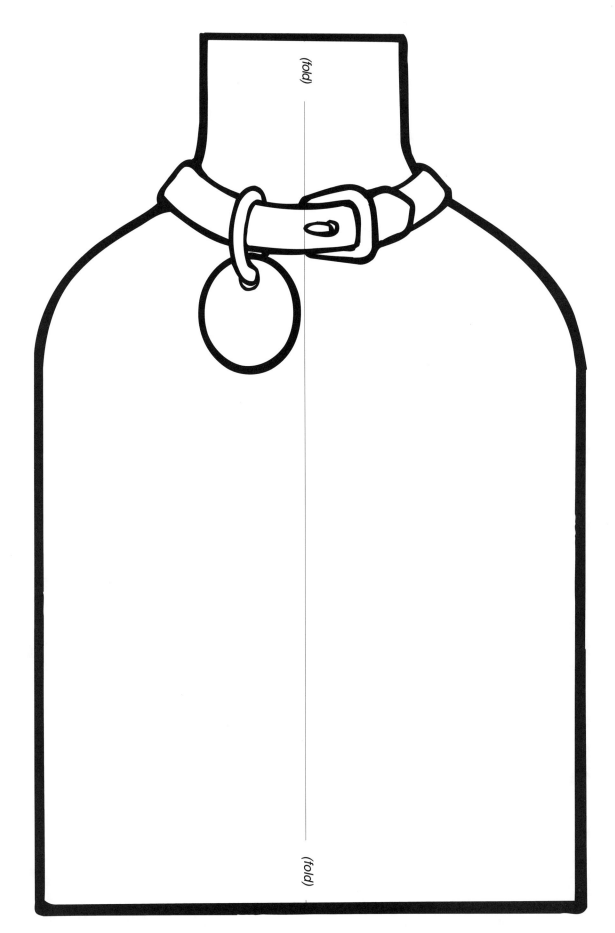

(fold)

(fold)

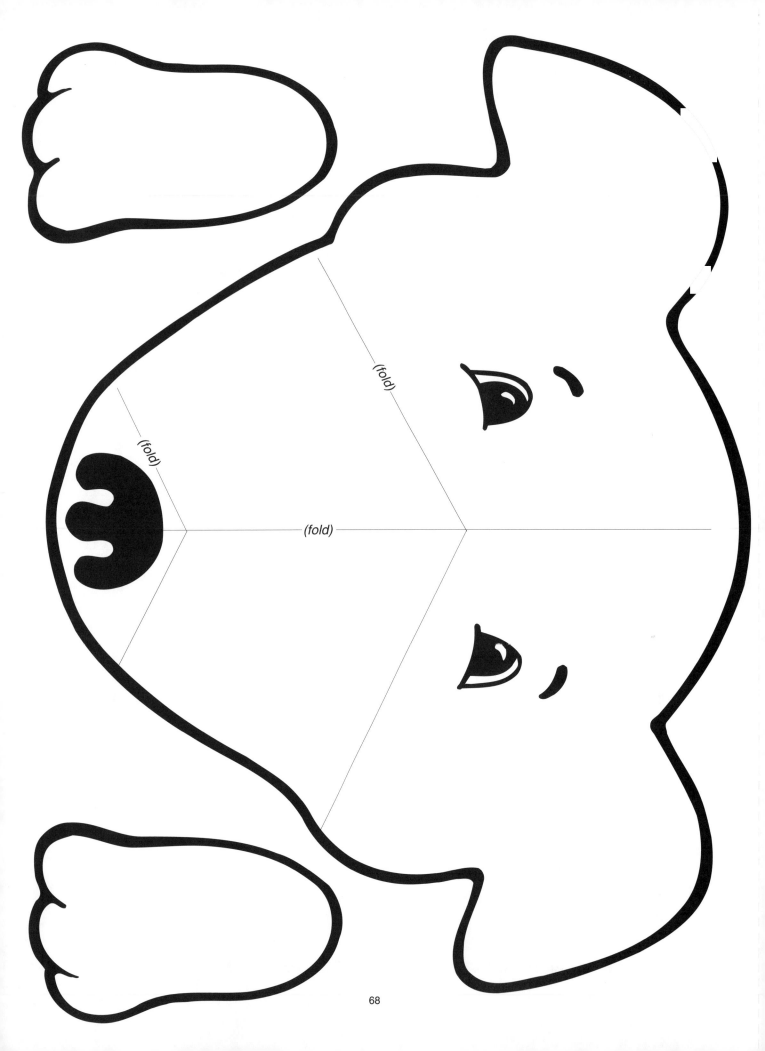

(fold)

(fold)

(fold)

The Cookie

A Three-Part Book

Materials

Individual books:

- 7" x 18" (18 x 45.5 cm) brown construction paper
- 3 copies of the writing form on page 72
- scissors, glue
- crayons or felt pens

1 Fold the construction paper. Trim the top and bottom to create the cookie shape.

Cut the three writing forms.

2 What kind of cookie is this? Draw chocolate chips, raisins, or decorations on the cookie.

Print the title of the story.

3

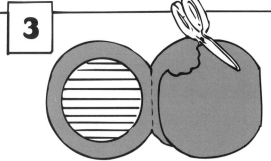

Unfold the first layer. Make it look like someone took a bite from the corner of the second layer. Glue a writing paper on the facing page.

4

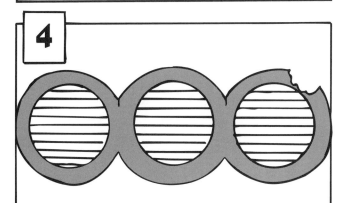

Unfold the second layer. Glue two more story sheets in these sections.

Literature Connections

The Chocolate Chip Cookie Contest by Barbara Douglas; Lothrop, Lee & Shepard Books, 1985.

A boy learns to bake chocolate chip cookies and wins a prize.

The Doorbell Rang by Pat Hutchins; Greenwillow, 1986.

Each time the doorbell rings, more friends come to share the cookies.

Frog and Toad Together by Arnold Lobel; Harper & Row, 1972.

One chapter in this chapter book addresses the idea of will-power and cookies.

If You Give a Mouse a Cookie by Laura Joffe Numeroff; Harper & Row, 1985.

If you give a mouse a cookie, he'll need lots of other things too.

My Grandmother's Cookie Jar by Montcalee Miller; Price Stern Sloan, 1987.

Grandma passes on stories of her Indian people as she shares cookies with her grandchild.

Ruth's Bake Shop by Kate Spohn; Orchard Books, 1990.

An octopus loves to bake, so she opens her own bake shop.

Who Stole the Cookies? by Judith Moffatt; Grosset & Dunlap, 1996.

One by one the animals deny stealing the cookies, until the real thief is found.

Writing Connections

Who Stole the Cookies?

Solve the mystery of the disappearing cookies. Write about what you think really happened.

My Favorite Cookie

Describe your favoite cookie and tell why you like it best.

Invent a New Cookie

Develop a new cookie. Name it and write a recipe for its preparation.

The Cookie

I slowly lift the lid
And stick my hand right in.
I can smell the chocolate.
My mouth begins to grin.
I grab the one on top
And pull it from the jar.
My dad's home-baked cookies
Are the very best by far.

Jill Norris

Something More to Do...

Make Cookies

1. Use your favorite recipe to make a batch of cookies with your class. Have students measure and mix to gain the experience that they need to write about making cookies.

2. As the cookies are baking, create a word bank of cookie words to use in writing.

3. Enjoy the warm cookies with a cold glass of milk and add a few more delicious words to the word bank.

Cookie Words

utensils

sift

measure

mix

stir

blend

mouth-watering

chewy

crunchy

Write a Cookbook

Have students bring copies of their favorite cookie recipes. Reproduce the recipes and create a *Cookie Cookbook*. These cookbooks make terrific gifts for classroom helpers.

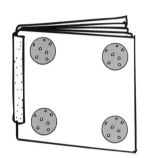

Play the *Who Stole the Cookies* Game?

1. Alternate clapping and hitting your legs as you chant:

All:	*Who stole the cookies from the cookie jar?*
Leader:	*_____ stole the cookies from the cookie jar.*
Person named:	*Who me?*
All:	*Yes, you.*
Person named:	*Couldn't be.*
All:	*Then who?*
Person named:	*_____ stole the cookies from the cookie jar.*

2. Repeat until all have had a chance to be named. The last person called is "in the cookie jar" and will start the game as the leader the next time it is played.

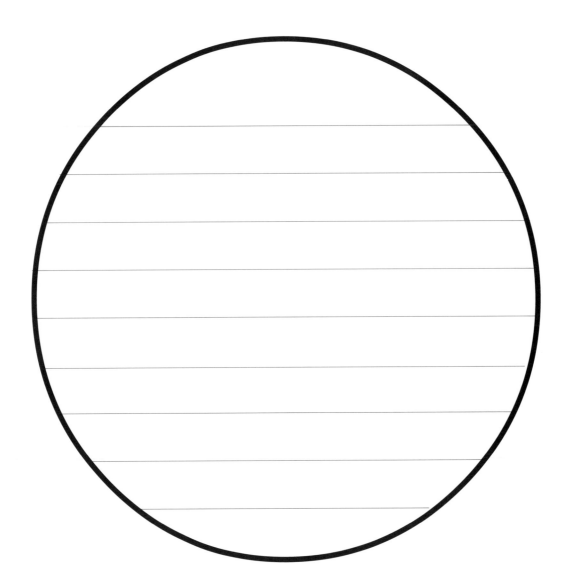

The Cave

A Three-Part Book

Materials

Individual books:

- 7" x 18" (18 x 45.5 cm) brown construction paper
- scraps of colored construction paper
- 3 copies of the writing form on page 76
- scissors, glue
- crayons or felt pens

1 Fold the construction paper. Trim the top to create the cave shape.

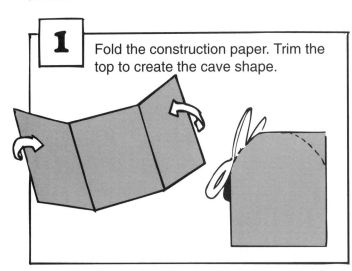

2 Make the cave opening with paper scraps or felt pen.

Print the title of the story.

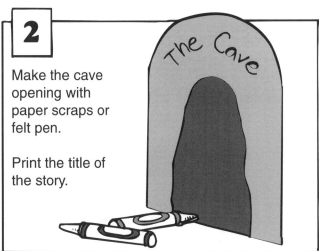

3

Unfold the first layer. Make the cave opening again. What is that peering out now? Glue a writing paper on the facing page.

4

Open the last layer. Glue two more story sheets in these sections. Use this space to write a story about the surprise inside the cave.

Literature Connections

Fiction Books:

Alone in the Caves by Eleonore Schmid; North-South Books, 1986.

Two children explore a cave and have some scary moments.

The Bear's Cave by Regine Schindler; Dutton Children's Books, 1988.

Rabbit and Mouse spend winter with Bear in his cave.

Nonfiction Books:

Caves and Caverns by Gail Gibbons; Harcourt Brace & Company, 1993.

Mammoth Cave National Park by Ruth Radlauer; Children's Press, 1985

One Small Square—Cave by Donald M. Silver; W. H. Freeman & Co., 1993.

What's in the Cave? by Peter Seymore; Holt, Rinehart & Winston, 1985.

The World Beneath Your Feet by Judith E. Rinehard; National Geographic Society, 1985.

Writing Connections

Strange Eyes in the Dark

What strange creatures belong to those glowing eyes?

My Home, the Cave

What would your life be like if you lived in a cave? Describe a day.

The Crowded Cave

Write an add-on story using a cave as the home. Start with one cave dweller and add one more on each page until the cave can't accommodate any more. What happens then?

**Dark and damp,
Light the lamp.**

**Cool and quiet,
We can try it.**

**Carefully
As can be.**

**Side by side,
Crawl inside.**

**We'll be brave
In our cave.**

Jill Norris

Something More to Do...

Build a Classroom Cave

If you and your students are ready for a challenging project, build a cave in your classroom. Make it large enough for young scientists to crawl into.

After reading about caves, make three-dimensional models of cave animals and geological formations to place in the cave. Use the bat pattern below to create hanging bats.

Here are some suggested ways you might create such a cave:

1. two refrigerator boxes taped together

2. a tarp, blanket, or dark sheet draped over moveable room dividers, a tall table, or bookcases set at an angle.

3. an old tent painted to look like a cave

Use the brilliant ideas originating in the minds of your students.

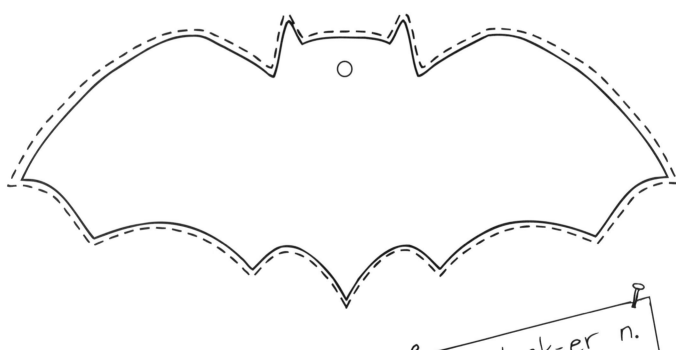

Review Safety Rules for Spelunking

After reading Silver's *One Small Square — Cave* and other nonfiction articles, write a set of rules for exploring caves. Post the rules outside of your class cave. If there are caves in your community, make sure that students understand the rules and restrictions about their exploration.

spe-lunk-er n.
a cave explorer

75

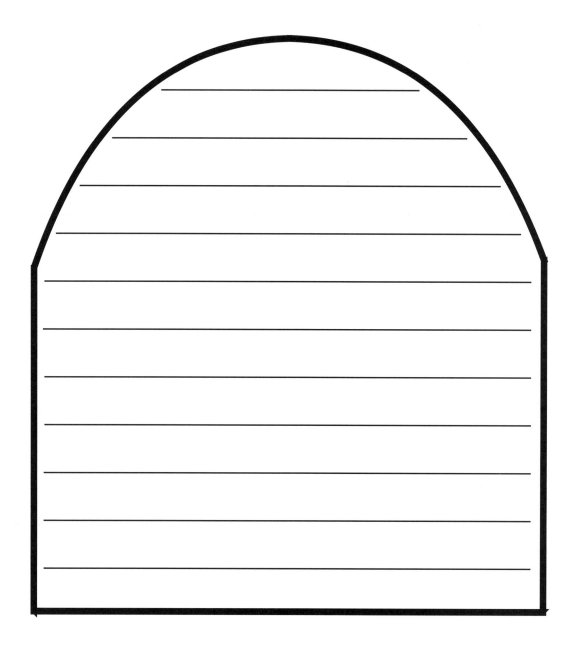

How to Make Books with Children EMC 777

My Bear

A Flap Book

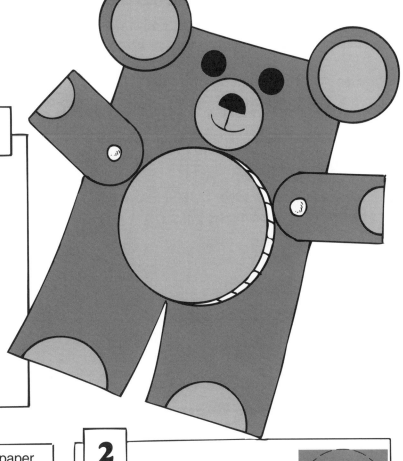

1

Fold the large brown construction paper in half two times.

Cut the bottom panel up the center to the first fold.

2

Round the corners on all pink and brown squares to make circles.

Cut one 4" pink and 3" pink in half.

Cut the 4" x 12" brown strip in half and cut rounded corners on one end of each half.

3

Glue on the circles.

Attach the arms with paper fasteners.

Add eyes and a nose cut from black paper.

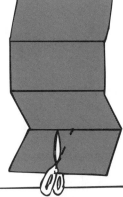

4

Staple the writing pages together, using the 7" pink circle as the cover. Glue the book to the bear's tummy.

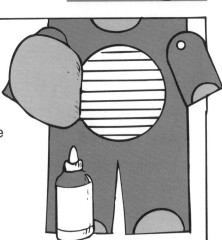

Literature Connections

The Bear on the Moon **by Joanne Ryder; Morrow Junior Books, 1991.**

A tale about how the great white bears that live at the top of the world came to live on ice and snow.

Brown Bear, Brown Bear **by Bill Martin Jr.; Henry Holt & Company, 1967.**

Animals answer the question "What do you see?" in this familiar pattern book.

The Day Sun Was Stolen **by Jamie Oliviero; Hyperion Books, 1995.**

A Haida tale about why the bear hibernates and some other animals grow thick fur for winter months.

Every Autumn Comes the Bear **by Jim Arnosky; G. P. Putnam's Sons, 1993.**

This book reviews the routines of a bear in the fall before hibernation.

Somebody and the Three Blairs **by Marilyn Tolhurst; Orchard Books, 1990.**

A retelling of the traditional Goldilocks tale featuring a bear who visits the home of a human family.

Sometimes brown,
Sometimes white,
Sometimes black...
What a sight!

Sometimes fierce
In its lair,
Sometimes tame...
Teddy bear.

Jill Norris

Writing Connections

Dinner Time

What has little bear stuffed his tummy with this time?

Why I Love My Teddy Bear

Describe your bear and tell why it is special.

Bear Facts

What can you tell me about bears?

Why Do Bears _____?

Make up a story to tell why a bear does something that it does. (*The Day Sun Was Stolen* is a good example of this type of story.)

Something More to Do...

Take Home Mr. Bear

1. Prepare a take-home pack with a stuffed bear, several outfit changes, and a "diary" (this can be a blank book or a spiral notebook) in a bag that can be easily carried. Include a note in the front of the diary explaining the take-home pack.

2. Send the pack home with a different child each night. Students will dictate or write about their adventures with Mr. Bear.

3. Read the diary each day as the pack returns to school.

Dear Boys and Girls,

My name is Mr. Bear and this is my diary. When you take me home to spend the night, please write down what we did together. (You can tell your mom or your dad and they can help you write it.) Then I will always remember our special times together.

Love,
Mr. Bear

Dear Parents,

Each day one student in our room will be chosen to take Mr. Bear home to spend the night. Mr. Bear comes with a carrying bag, several different outfits, and a diary. Please help your student to record the things that Mr. Bear did while he was at your home. Send Mr. Bear back to school the following day and we will read about his exciting adventures.

Thanks for your support,

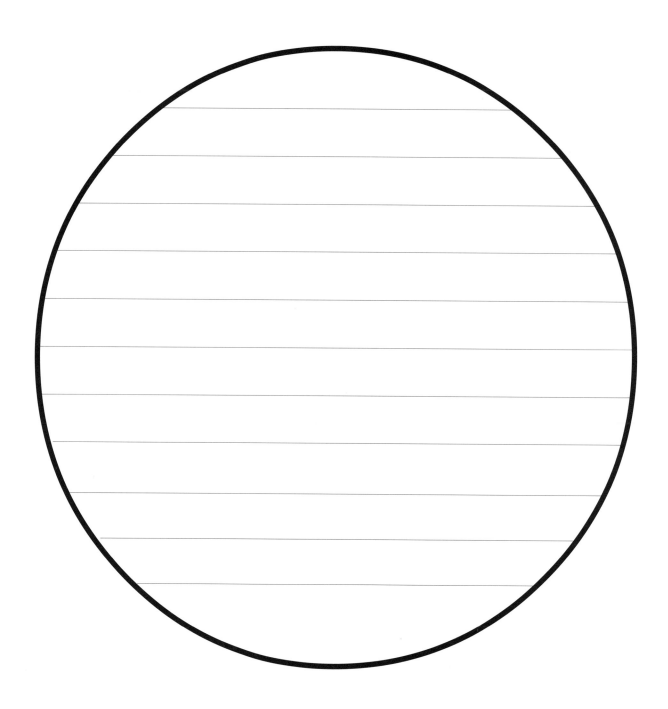

How to Make Books with Children EMC 777

What's Under the Bed?

A Flap Book

Materials

Class book or individual book:

- 12" x 18" (30.5 x 45.5 cm) construction paper
- the reproducible form on page 84
- writing paper
- scissors, stapler
- felt pens or crayons
- glue

1

Have students draw their faces on the pillows on the reproducible forms.

Color the picture.

2

Cut out the form. Cut the two slits at the bottom of the bed. Fold up the flap. Glue the bed to the construction paper.

Lift the flap and draw the surprise.

3 Glue completed story papers on the left side of the construction paper.

4 Bind the book for each student or compile all the stories for a class book.

What's Under the Bed

Literature Connections

***Don't Wake Up Mama* by Eileen Christelow; Clarion, 1992.**

Five little monkeys try to bake a cake for their mother's birthday without waking her up.

***Go to Bed* by Virginia Miller; Candlewick Press, 1993.**

In this story, little bear resists going to bed.

***The Napping House* by Audrey Wood; Harcourt Brace Jovanovich, 1984.**

A flea wakes up a pile of sleeping creatures with just one bite.

***The Princess and the Pea* retold by Sucie Stevenson; Doubleday, 1992.**

A young girl proves that she is a real princess by feeling a pea through twenty mattresses and twenty feather beds.

***There's an Alligator Under My Bed* by Mercer Mayer; Dial Books, 1987.**

The alligator under the bed makes a boy's bedtime hazardous.

***There's a Monster Under My Bed* by James Howe; Atheneum, 1986.**

Simon is sure that there are monsters under his bed. What can he do?

***What's Under My Bed?* by James Stevenson; Greenwillow, 1983.**

Grandpa remembers when he was afraid at bedtime and reassures his grandchildren.

***The Underbed* by Cathryn Clinton Hoellwarth; Good Books, 1990.**

A little boy and his mother check under his bed for a disturbing creature called "the underbed."

Writing Connections

My Jiggling Bed

I was sleeping peacefully when suddenly my bed began to jiggle. Tell why the bed jiggled and what you did.

Under My Bed

If you looked under my bed, you would see... Write a nonfiction account of what is really under your bed, then write a fiction account. Which one do you like better?

Noises from Down Under

A strange noise began to come from under _____'s bed. Tell whose bed it is and what is causing the noise. Write a story to tell what happened next.

Each sunny morning when I wake

I check beneath my bed

For magic dreams that might be there.

Today, I found my socks instead!

Jill Norris

Something More to Do...

Write a Procedure for Going to Bed

1. Discuss with your class the routines that they follow when they go to bed.

2. On the form below, have students dictate or write all the different things that they do in the correct order.

3. Make a "pillow" from two sheets of white construction paper. Staple the sheets together around the edges, leaving a small opening for stuffing. Stuff the "pillow" with bits of newspaper. Staple the opening closed.

4. Attach the *Going To Bed Procedure* to the "pillow" with a big safety pin.

Who's Under the Bed?

1. Prepare a bed by covering a table with a sheet to hide what is underneath.

2. Have one student leave the room while another student hides under the "bed."

3. The student returns from outside the room and sits on the "bed" while guessing who is underneath.

4. Students in the "audience" can give clues to help.

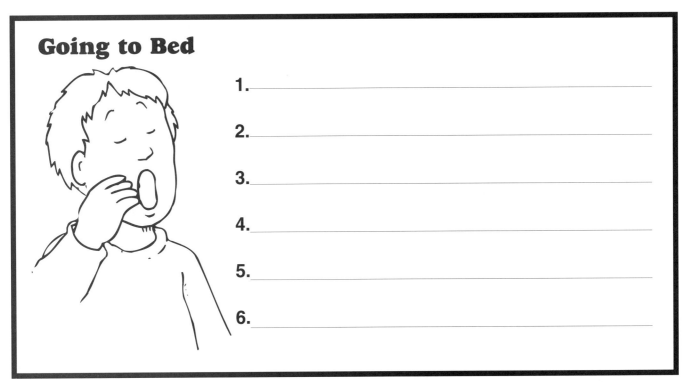

Going to Bed

1. _____

2. _____

3. _____

4. _____

5. _____

6. _____

 How to Make Books with Children EMC 777

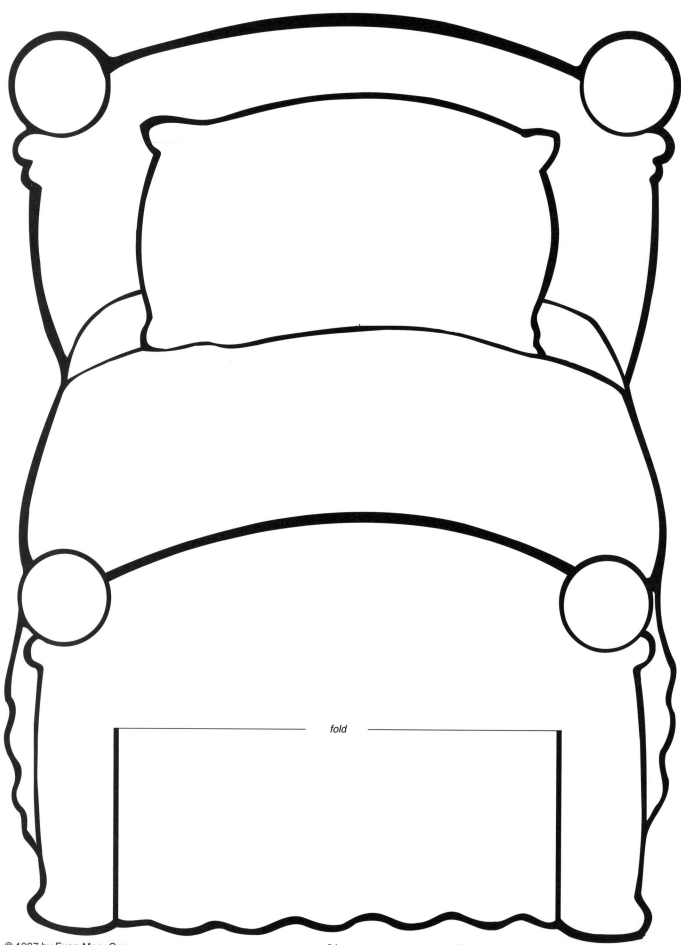

fold

How to Make Books with Children EMC 777

The Crocodile
A Flap Book

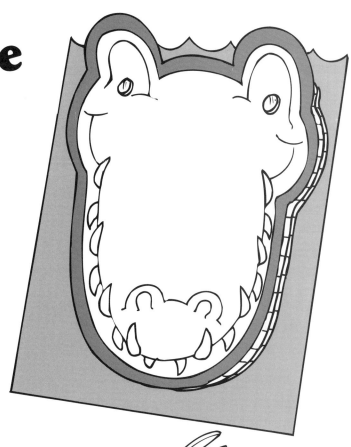

1

Cut out and color the crocodile pattern.

Glue the pattern to the green paper and cut it out, leaving a small border of green showing.

2

Cut a wave pattern across one end of the blue tagboard. This is the back cover.

3

Fold the top of the crocodile pattern down on the fold line.

Cut writing paper to match the shape.

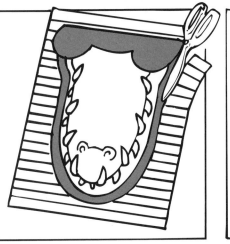

4

Assemble book by pushing paper fasteners through all layers at eye.

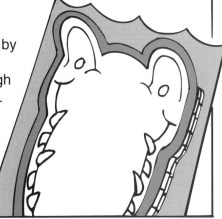

How to Make Books with Children EMC 777

Literature Connections

Bill and Pete Go Down the Nile **by Tomie dePaola; G. P. Putnam's Sons, 1987.**

William Everett Crocodile and his friend encounter a jewel thief at the museum.

Elephant Pie **by Hilda Offen; Dutton Children's Books, 1993.**

The cherry pie for Mrs. Snipper-Snapper's birthday causes some problems.

The Enormous Crocodile **by Roald Dahl; Alfred A. Knopf, 1978.**

This book is filled with secret plans and clever tricks.

Five Little Monkeys Sitting in a Tree **by Eileen Christelow; Clarion Books, 1991.**

Five little monkeys tease Mr. Crocodile as he swims under their tree.

Ten Little Crocodiles **by Colin West; Barron's, 1988.**

Count down with the crocodiles in this book.

Writing Connections

Crocodile's Smile

Why is crocodile so happy? Does he have a secret?

The Great Escape

Poor crocodile has been captured. If he doesn't escape soon, he'll be put in a zoo. Help him to get away.

Surprise

You are walking along the river and you meet a crocodile.

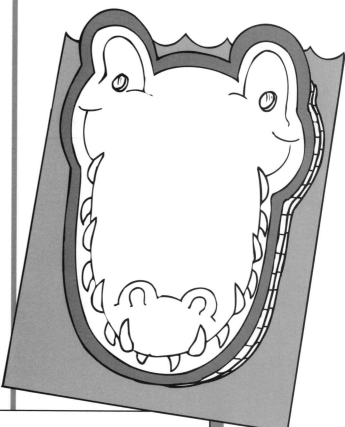

Alligator has a broad, broad nose;
Crocodile's is long and thin.
But both of them are dangerous
When they begin to grin.

Jo Ellen Moore

Something More to Do...

Make a Crocodile Gulper

Materials:
- two strips of stiff poster board
  1 1/2" x 8" (3.5 x 20 cm)
- crocodile head and jaw patterns
- 3/4" paper fastener

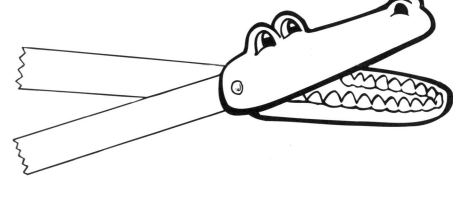

What to Do:
1. Reproduce the crocodile head and jaw patterns below.
2. Color and cut out the crocodile and punch holes where indicated.
3. Punch a hole 2" (5 cm) from one end of each posterboard strip.
4. Glue each part of the crocodile to a strip, matching holes.
5. Secure the two strips with paper fastener.
6. Use the gulper as a shadow puppet or as a giant pointer:
   - Gulp little fish to demonstrate subtraction.
   - Point out letters or words from a word list.
   - Choose students to line up.

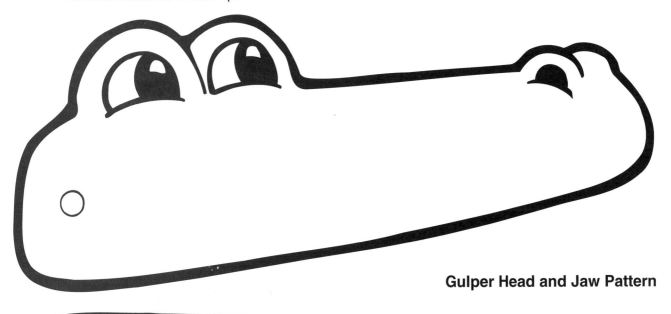

Gulper Head and Jaw Pattern

   How to Make Books with Children EMC 777

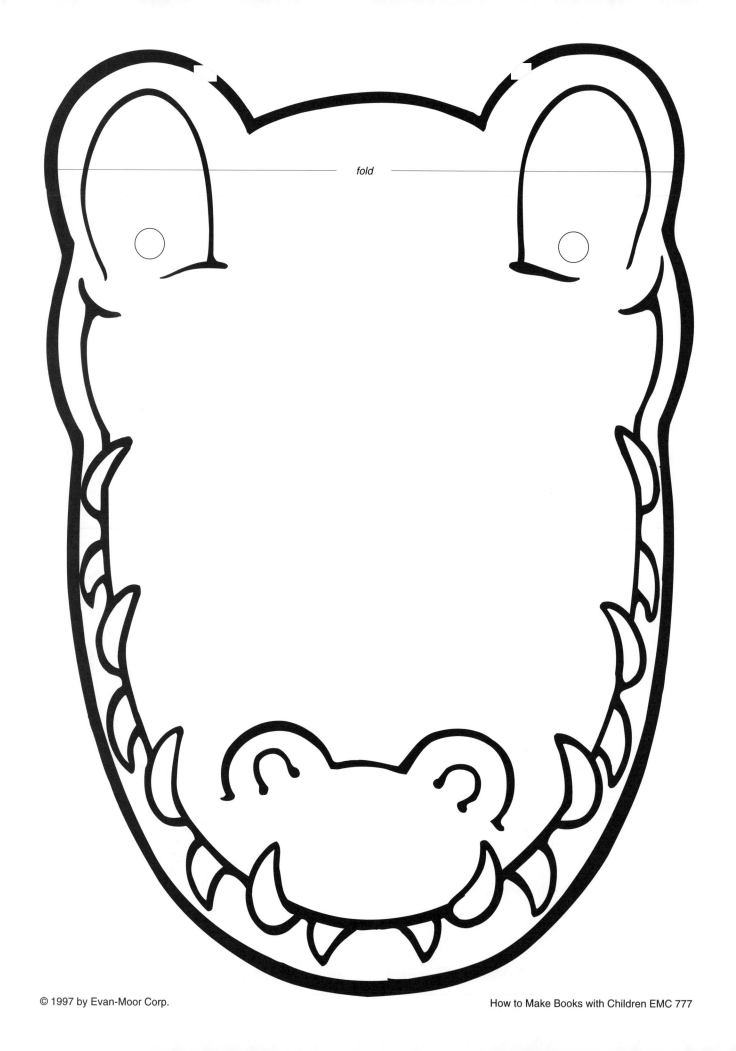

fold

How to Make Books with Children EMC 777

What's in the Cupboard?

A Flap Book

Class book:

- reproducible pattern on page 92
- 12" x 18" (30.5 x 45.5 cm) construction paper
- cupboard doors
    - 2" x 5 1/2" (5 x 14 cm) paper
    - 3" x 5 1/2" (5 x 14 cm) paper
- writing paper
- 2 paper fasteners
- scissors, glue
- stapler
- felt pens or crayons

1

Cut out and color the reproducible. Draw something inside the top and bottom sections of the cupboard.

2

Glue the cupboard on one half of the construction paper and the writing paper on the other half.

3

Cut cupboard doors in half.

Make a narrow fold on the end of each door. Glue this strip to the cupboard so doors can open and close.

4

For a class book, place all student pages together. Add a decorated cover and staple. Glue a folded paper strip over the staples.

Paper fasteners can be used as cupboard pulls.

How to Make Books with Children EMC 777

Literature Connections

But No Candy by Gloria Houston; Philomel Books, 1992.

During World War II, a little girl is disappointed because there is no candy on the shelves of her father's store.

China Shelf Luxury by Lily Troia; Raintree, 1990.

A mouse family enjoys the life in a china cupboard.

The Lily Cupboard by Shulamith Levey Oppenheim; Harper & Row, 1992.

Miriam, a young Jewish girl, must leave her parents to hide with strangers in the country during World War II.

Pots and Pans by Anne Rockwell; Macmillan, 1993.

This easy picture book shows the objects in a kitchen cupboard.

Teeny Tiny by Jill Bennett; G. P. Putnam's Sons, 1986.

A teeny-tiny women puts a teeny-tiny bone in her cupboard.

Writing Connections

In Grandma's Cupboard

Grandma always has interesting things on her cupboard shelf. Today we found...

Old Mother Hubbard's Cupboard

Her cupboard was empty, so she went shopping. What is on the shelf now?

The Ancient Cabinet

I bought an old cabinet at the auction. What do you think I will find when I open the doors?

I open the doors very carefully:
Tiny china cups and a teapot fine,
Fancy dollies dressed in wide-brimmed hats,
A rocking chair hand-carved from pine,
A pair of spectacles used long ago,
From across the sea, a miniature sword.
The shelves are filled with treasures...
My grandmother's corner cupboard.

Jill Norris

Something More to Do...

What's in the Cupboard?

Before You Begin
Make a "door" that you can attach to a bulletin board or chalkboard. This will be your cupboard door. You will change the things in your cupboard and then open the door to reveal what is inside. Use pictures or real items to represent categories of things that could be in your cupboard.

How to Play
Put several items behind the cupboard door. The object of the game is to identify the "rule of the cupboard" after viewing the items.

Open the door to the cupboard and show the things inside to the class. Say, "All the things in this cupboard are alike in some way. Can you tell me how they are alike?" Allow students to suggest attributes. As guesses are made, check them. Example: "I think all the things in the cupboard have a lid." Check the objects to see if the guess is correct.

Explain that the "rule of the cupboard" is the thing that is alike about each item in the cupboard. When the rule has been identified, take several new items, show them to the class, and ask if they could go in the cupboard. Students will check to see if they follow the cupboard's rule and decide whether they can be put inside.

Change the items inside and work with students to discover the new cupboard's rule. Continue until students are comfortable with the procedure.

Extension
Extend the game by creating a *Cupboard Big Book*. Create pages similar to the bulletin board pictured above. Students will draw several items in their cupboard. Have students list the items in their cupboards and ask the question "What is the rule for this cupboard?" The rule can be written on the back of the page.

Allow time for students to share their pages with the class and guess the cupboard rules. Bind the pages into a class big book. The cover should give readers directions for enjoying the book.

- Open the cupboard door on each page in this book.
- Look at the things in the cupboard.
- Try to find out what is alike about all of the things.
- Then guess the rule for putting things in that cupboard.

91 How to Make Books with Children EMC 777

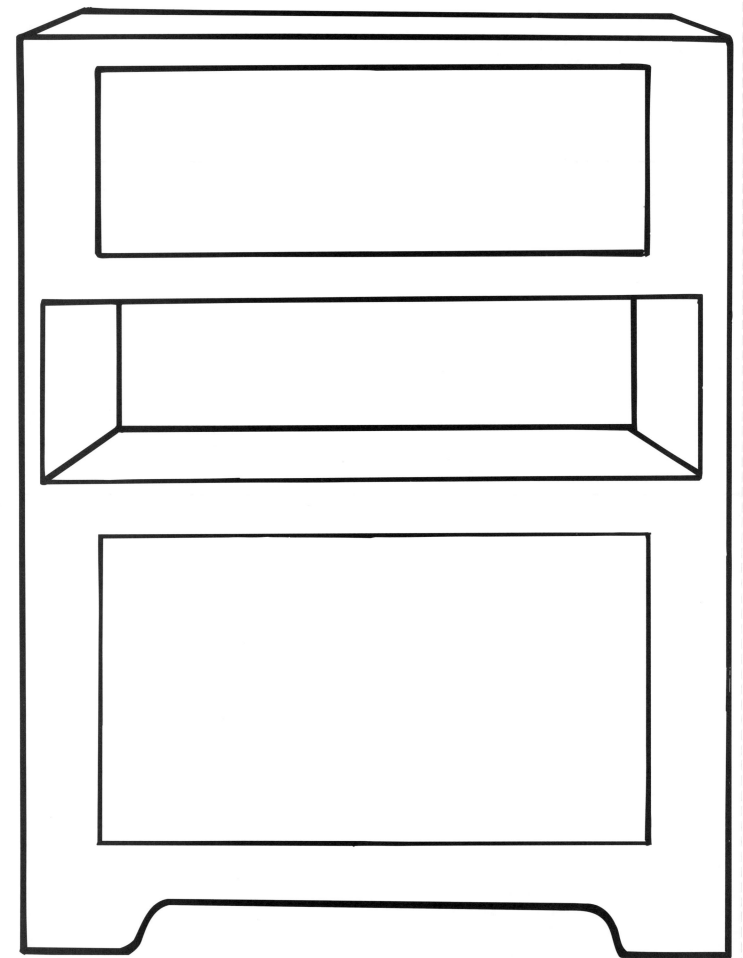

How to Make Books with Children EMC 777

The Duck
A Flap Book

Class book:

- 2 sheets of 9" x 12" (23 x 30.5 cm) yellow construction paper
- reproducible patterns on pages 95 and 96
- 1 strip of 1/2" x 5" (3.75 x 13 cm) yellow construction paper
- writing paper
- stapler
- scissors, glue
- felt pens or crayons

Individual Book:

The patterns on pages 95 and 96 can also be used to make individual books.

1 Cut out and color the duck pattern. Glue it to a yellow paper to make the book cover.

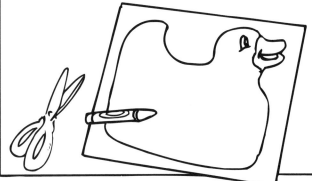

2 Put both sheets of yellow paper together and cut, leaving some yellow showing.

3 Give a duck pattern to each student. Add writing lines before reproducing. Students write a riddle about what is under the duck's wing.

Glue on the wing pattern.
Hide the answer to the riddle under the wing.

4

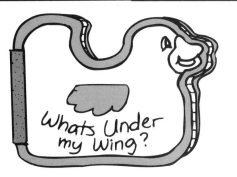

Staple writing pages inside the covers. Glue the strip of yellow paper over the staples.

Literature Connections

***Chibi: A True Story from Japan* by Barbara Brenner and Julia Takaya; Houghton Mifflin, 1995**

A brave mother duck raises her family in a busy city.

***Farmer Duck* by Martin Waddell; Candlewick Press, 1992.**

A kind, hardworking duck needs the help of the other animals to take care of the farm.

***Five Little Ducks* by Ian Beck; Henry Holt & Company, 1992.**

Mother Duck searches for her missing ducklings.

***Ikotmi and the Ducks* by Paul Goble; Orchard Books, 1990.**

A trickster tale about why some ducks have red eyes.

***Make Way for Ducklings* by Robert McCloskey; Viking, 1941.**

In this Caldecott winner, Mr. and Mrs. Mallard make a nest and raise their ducklings in the Boston Commons.

Mother Duck leads the parade.

    Quack, Quack, Waddle, Waddle

    Quack, Quack, Waddle, Waddle

Each fuzzy duckling is displayed.

    Quack, Quack, Waddle, Waddle

    Quack, Quack, Waddle, Waddle

They march along with heads held high.

    Quack, Quack, Waddle, Waddle

    Quack, Quack, Waddle, Waddle

Nodding to each passerby.

    Quack, Quack, Waddle, Waddle

    Quack, Quack, Waddle, Waddle

Jill Norris

Writing Connections

What's Under My Wing

Write a riddle about what is hiding under a duck's wing. Draw a picture of the answer under the lift-up wing.

Help Me!

Imagine that you are a duckling and you are afraid of the water. What will you do? Lessons? Life preserver? Write about your dilemma and how you solve it.

Dabblers

The ducks you see in ponds are dabblers. They put their heads in the water and their tails in the air and paddle as fast as they can. They are feeding on weeds and water plants. Write about something unusual that the duck might see as it is dabbling and what happens because of this unusual event.

The Little Lost Duck

Mother Duck has lost her duckling. Write about where the duckling is and how Mother Duck finds it.

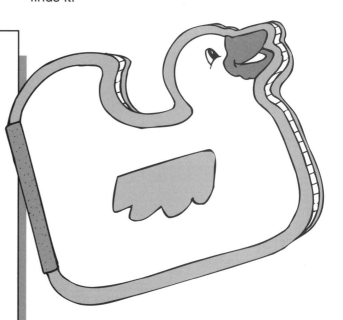

Something More to Do...

A Duck Parade

1. Teach your class the duck parade poem or learn a duck song like "Little Ducky Duddle" or "Five White Ducks."

2. Make duck-bill visors out of a 6" x 9" (15 x 23 cm) piece of tagboard. Attach a large rubber band to the visor with two paper clips.

3. Practice the the duck walk. (Squat on the floor with hands under armpits to form wings. Waddle forward.)

4. Now, put on the visors, recite the poem, and waddle forward.

5. Videotape this performance for future viewing!!

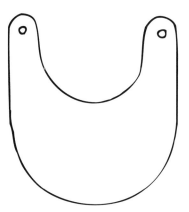

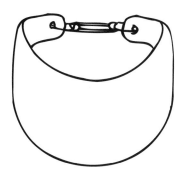

Learning about Ducks

After reading several books about ducks to your class, lead the class in a discussion of what ducklings might be saying to each other as they swim about in the pond. (Be sure to include both nonfiction and fiction selections.)

Select several students to be ducks on the pond and listen to their conversation, or have students write a dialogue for a pair of ducks.

Pattern for the Duck's Wing

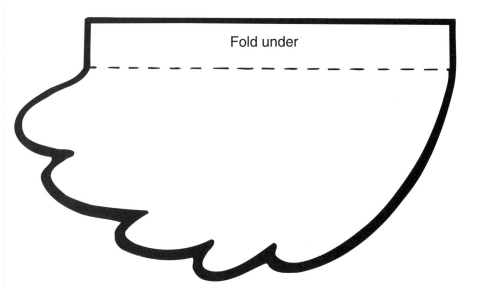

Fold under

     How to Make Books with Children EMC 777

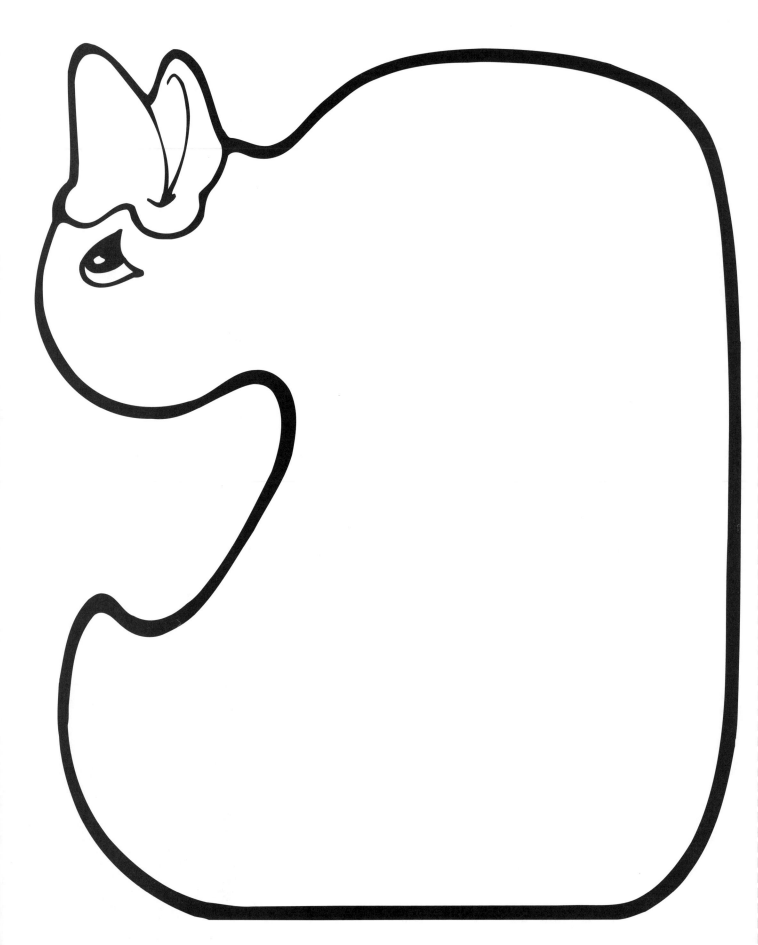

How to Make Books with Children EMC 777

The Alien

A Flap Book

Materials

Class or individual book:

- 1 sheet each blue and yellow 12" x 12" (30.5 x 30.5 cm) construction paper
- reproducible pattern from page 100
- writing paper
- silver star stickers or star patterns on page 100
- scissors, glue
- blue ribbon, hole punch
- felt pens or crayons

---

1 Color and cut out the alien pattern. Fold the "arms" on the fold line.

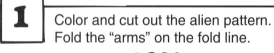

2 Cut the front cover from the yellow paper.

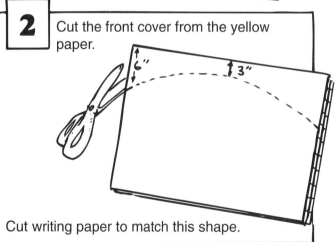

Cut writing paper to match this shape.

---

3 Staple writing paper to blue paper. Glue alien to blue paper as shown.

Place stars randomly.

4 Put all layers together and punch holes. Tie together with blue ribbon.

His arms fold down over the yellow paper.

Give the book a title.

Literature Connections

It Came from Outer Space by Tony Bradman; Dial Books, 1992.

A visitor from space drops in on an elementary school.

Space Out! Jokes about Outer Space by Peter and Connie Roop; Lerner Publications, 1984.

This is a book of space riddles.

The Magic School Bus Lost in the Solar System by Joanna Cole; Scholastic, 1990.

Miss Frizzle and her class take a field trip through the solar system.

Moog-Moog, Space Barber by Mark Teague; Scholastic, 1990.

Elmo gets a terrible haircut and makes a trip to outer space to get it fixed.

Alistar and the Alien Invasion by Marilyn Sadler; Simon & Schuster, 1994.

Alistar saves the earth from an alien invasion.

June 29, 1999 by David Wiesner; Clarion Books, 1992.

Vegetables from outer space and a third grade science project combine in this imaginative tale.

Writing Connections

A Postcard Home

Compose a postcard that an alien might send home describing his visit to Earth.

Mysterious Visitors from Space

Who is coming over the hill? What will happen when the space visitors and earthlings meet?

Escape from Danger

Strange events have been occurring to the astronauts on the space station. What could be happening?

Little purple creatures
With shining, flashing eyes...
Five arms, three legs,
And wings like dragonflies...

When I imagine visitors
Who come from outer space,
I see strange unusual beings,
A real un-human race.

Jill Norris

Something More to Do...

Create an Alien

Complete this research project and then apply what you learn. Use the form on this page as a guide for students.

1. Choose a location in outer space like a moon or a particular planet. Find out about the conditions for life there.
    - Is it hot? Cold?
    - Is there gravity? How much?
    - Is there oxygen to breathe? Water to drink?

2. After they have assessed the conditions for human life, have your students develop an alien that could survive there. Describe its adaptations and relate them to specific life processes.

Write a Guidebook for Alien Visitors

A group of aliens will be arriving at your school for a special exchange program. They have never been to Earth. What will they need to know? Write a guidebook to explain a day at school.

My alien has an insulated shell so that it can withstand very cold temperatures.

The Facts

place: _____

climate: _____

gravity: _____

oxygen: _____

water: _____

This is what I think an alien from this place would have to look like.

(fold)

(fold)

How to Make Books with Children EMC 777

What's in My Pocket?

A Flap Book

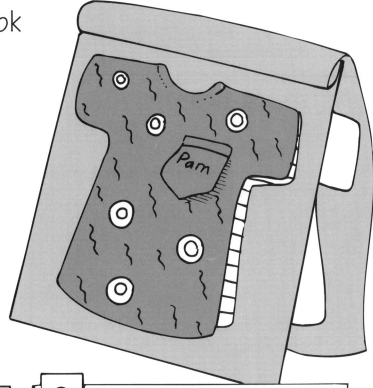

1 Choose a pocket shape and glue the flap only to the shirt.

Decorate the T-shirt (except under the pocket) and cut out.

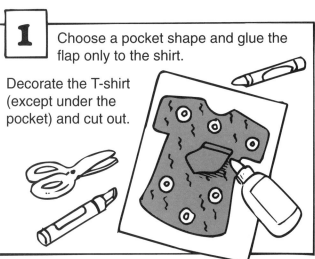

2 Cut writing paper to match the shirt shape.

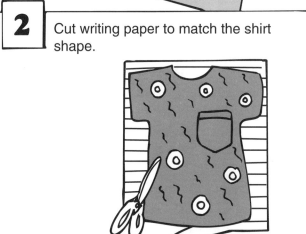

3 Glue the writing paper and the top edge of the shirt pattern to the construction paper.

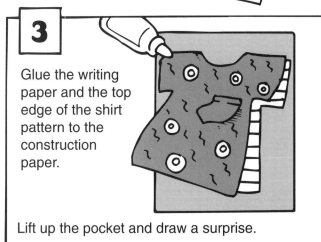

Lift up the pocket and draw a surprise.

4 Assemble student pages and bind together with a cover.

Secure at the top edge with buttons and thread.

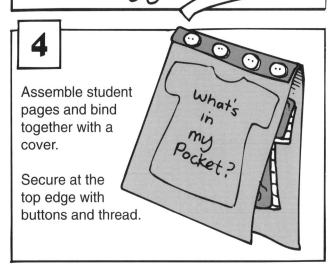

Literature Connections

Ohmygosh My Pocket by Janet Perry Marshall; Bell Books, 1992.

A young boy decides what to take to school in his pocket.

Peter's Pockets by Eve Rice; Greenwillow, 1989.

Peter's new pants don't have any pockets. What can he do?

A Pocket for Corduroy by Don Freeman; Viking, 1978.

Corduroy, the stuffed bear, gets a pocket for his overalls.

Rocks in my Pockets by Marc Harshman and Bonnie Collins; Cobblehill Books, 1991.

Members of the Woods Family may be poor, but they all have pockets and they all have rocks.

There's a Wocket in my Pocket by Dr. Seuss; Random House, 1974.

Rhyme and imagination fill this Dr. Seuss classic.

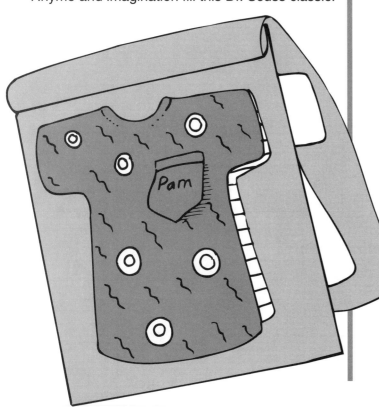

Writing Connections

The _____ in My Pocket

Tell about something that you found and put in your pocket. What will you do with it? What will happen when your mom finds it?

A Riddle in My Pocket

Write your riddle. Draw the answer under the pocket flap.

A Hole!

You put your lucky nickel and your lunch money in your pocket, and when you got to school the only thing in your pocket was a hole. Write about what happened. Did you find the missing things?

My shirt has one.

My pants have two.

My jacket, five.

How many on you?

P · O · C · K · E · T · S

You see them on hats

And even on shoes,

Aprons and purses,

And big kangaroos.

P · O · C · K · E · T · S

Fill 'em up.

Dump 'em out.

Count 'em now

As we shout.

P · O · C · K · E · T · S

Pockets!

Jill Norris

Something More to Do...

Count the Pockets

Create a graph showing the number of pockets that each person has.

1. Do a pocket count.

2. Record the results on a grid.

3. Analyze the graph.
   - Who has the most pockets?
   - Who has the least?
   - How many more pockets
     does _____ have than _____?

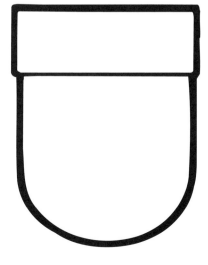

A Pocket Message Center

A pocket for each student in your class is like a mini-post office.

1. Give each student a 5" x 7" (13 x 18 cm) rectangle. You may use cloth, notecards, construction paper, or pieces of paper bags. Students should decorate their pockets and label them clearly.

2. Laminate the pockets and staple them to a small bulletin board. Leave the top open to slip things inside.

3. Use the pockets to:
   - designate helper jobs
   - send messages
   - take roll and lunch count

Pocket Patterns

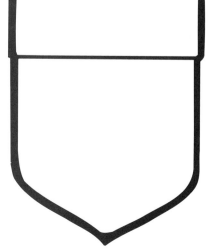

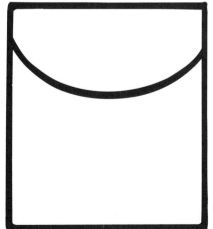

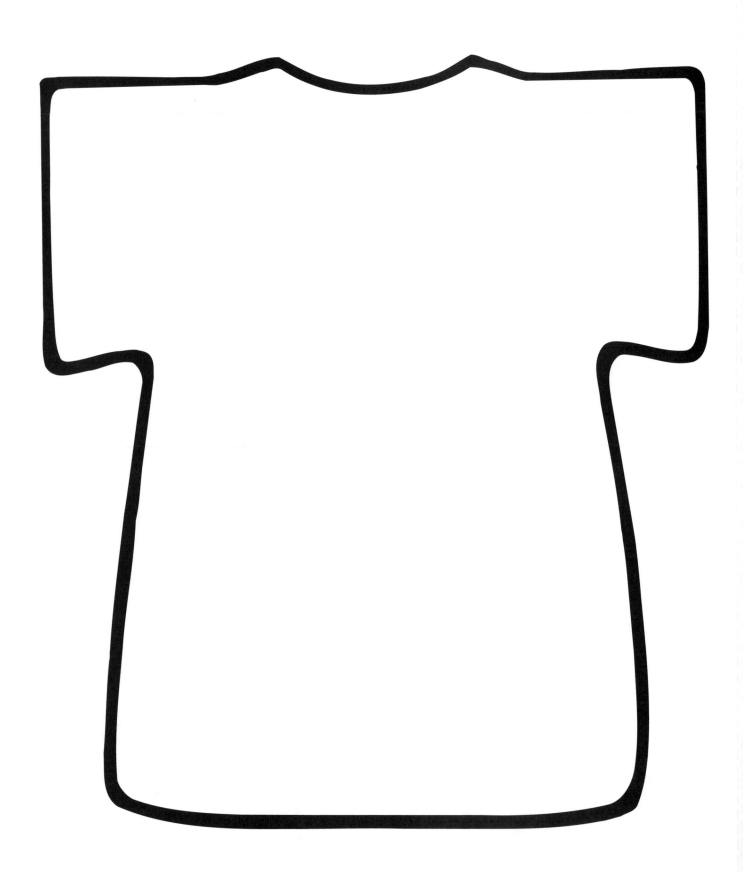

How to Make Books with Children EMC 777

The Whale

A Flap Book

Class or individual book:

- 12" x 18" (30.5 x 45.5 cm) sheet of blue construction paper
- reproducible patterns on pages 107-108
- 2" x 6" (5 x 15 cm) strip of black paper
- writing paper
- stapler
- scissors, glue
- felt pens or crayons

1 Cut 6" (15 cm) off the end of the blue paper.

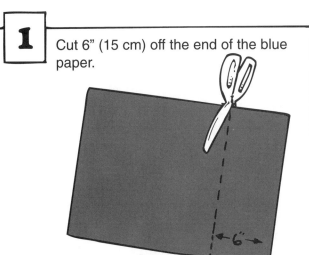

2 Cut a wave pattern across the smaller blue paper.

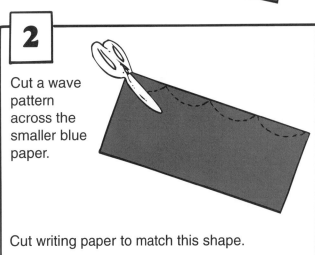

Cut writing paper to match this shape.

3 Assemble the finished stories and covers. Staple on the left side.

Glue the whale to the back cover.

4 Squeeze out white glue to make the spouting water. Let it dry thoroughly.

Fold the strip of black paper. Glue it around the binding. Cut out the title and glue to cover.

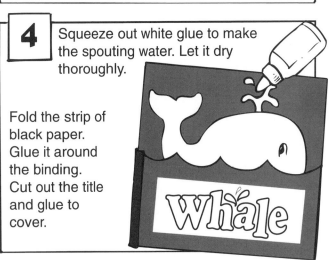

How to Make Books with Children EMC 777

Literature Connections

***Baby Beluga* by Raffi; Crown Publishers, 1980.**

The illustrated text of Raffi's song about the little white whale who swims wild and free.

***Going on a Whale Watch* by Bruce McMillan; Scholastic, 1992.**

Photographs show two six-year-olds on a whale watching expedition.

***An Ocean World* by Peter Sis; Greenwillow, 1992.**

A wordless tale of a whale who sails new seas in search of a friend.

***Whale Is Stuck* by Karen Hayles and Charles Fuge; Simon & Schuster, 1992.**

When he leaps, Whale lands on an ice floe. The other Arctic animals try to get him back in the sea.

***The Whale's Song* by Dyan Sheldon; Dial Books, 1990.**

Lilly wants to hear a whale sing.

Writing Connections

A Day with Baby Blue

Describe a day in the life of a baby blue whale. What would you see? What would you do? Where would you go?

My Pet Whale

Imagine that you had a whale for a pet. What special accommodations would that require? Think about food, a place to sleep, the neighbors. Write a story to tell about your pet problems.

Migration

Write simple reports on the migration of whales.

We Like Whales

List two or three reasons why you like whales.

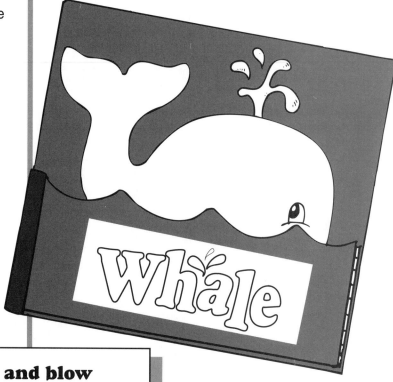

**Breech and blow
From below.
Watch it go....**

Jill Norris

Something More to Do...

Blubber as Insulation

Whales have a layer of fat called blubber just below their skin. This layer is like a thick blanket and helps to protect the whale from frigid water temperatures. Demonstrate the protective quality of blubber using rubber gloves and shortening.

Supplies:
- four rubber gloves
- tub of ice and water
- can of solid shortening

Before you begin:

1. Create an insulated glove, using two gloves and shortening.
   - Put one glove on your hand.
   - Cover it with a thick layer of shortening.
   - Cover the first glove and the shortening layer with another glove.

   You should have a shortening/glove sandwich. (glove-shortening layer-glove)

2. Put the remaining two gloves together. (glove-glove)

What to do:

Now challenge students to compare the two glove sets by placing their hands into the gloves and then into the icy water.
- Which glove, the shortening sandwich or the double glove, protected their hands better?
- How is the shortening sandwich glove like the whale?

Whale Cover Letters

       How to Make Books with Children EMC 777

The Eagle
An Accordion Book

Materials

Individual or small group book:

- 2 sheets of 9" x 12" (23 x 30.5 cm) black construction paper
- eagle pattern on page 112
- writing paper pattern on page 111
- tape
- scissors, glue
- felt pens or crayons

1 Fold the black sheets of paper to 6" x 9" (15 x 25 cm). Tape them together.

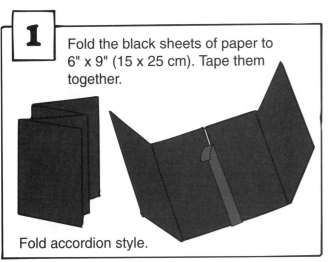

Fold accordion style.

2 Color and cut out the eagle pattern. Glue the eagle on the front section of the accordion-folded paper.

3 Cut the top of the black paper to match the shape of the eagle's head.

4 Glue the writing forms on each accordion folded segment.

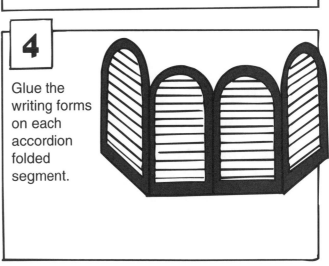

How to Make Books with Children EMC 777

Literature Connections

Brother Eagle, Sister Sky: A Message from Chief Seattle illustrated by **Susan Jeffers; Dial Books, 1991.**

Respect and love for the earth are major themes in Chief Seattle's moving message.

Eagle Boy: A Traditional Navajo Legend retold by **Gerald Hausman; HarperCollins, 1996.**

A Native American tale about a young boy who learns the healing ways of eagles.

Eagle Dreams by **Sheryl McFarlane; Philomel Books, 1994.**

Robin finds a bald eagle with a broken wing and nurses it back to health.

Eagles by **Joe Ban Wormer; E. P. Dutton, 1985.**

Photographs and informative text describe the bald eagle and the golden eagle.

Eagles—Lions of the Sky by **Emery & Durga Bernhard; Holiday House, 1994.**

This nonfiction book compares eagles to lions.

Regal, the Golden Eagle by **Lars Klinting; R & S Books, 1988.**

Regal takes flying lessons.

**Majestically he sweeps down,
Then soars and turns, mid-air.
Eagle seems to rule the skies
As he glides here and there.**

Jill Norris

Writing Connections

Eagle Express

This eagle is carrying a message. Imagine what the message is. Where is eagle taking it? Who sent it?

The American Eagle

Why do you think that the eagle is one symbol of the U.S.A.? Write about your ideas.

How Much Longer?

Baby eaglet has been in the nest for 10 weeks. Write the argument it might use to convince its mother that it's time to leave home.

How to Make Books with Children EMC 777

Something More to Do...

Eagle Facts

1. Collect facts about eagles. Use a variety of reference sources—reference books, video laser discs, encyclopedias, CD-ROMs. Write the facts on large charts.

2. Now create real references so that your students can connect the eagle facts to their own world.
   For example:
   - **The golden eagle and bald eagle have a wing span of about 7 feet (2 meters).**
   Unroll a long strip of paper and measure off 7 feet. Draw the eagle's wings on the strip. Have students stand in the center of the strip and hold out their arms to compare the eagle's wing spand with their outstretched arms.
   - **The eggs of the eagle are about 3 inches (8 centimeters) long and about 2 inches (5 centimeters) across.**
   Measure a paper egg shape about this size. The egg must be warmed for about 40 days before it hatches. Begin a daily tally and continue until hatching—40 days!

Writing Paper Pattern

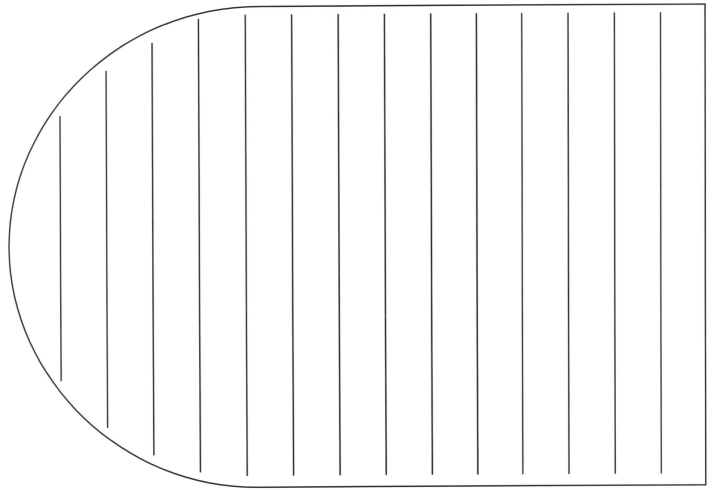

How to Make Books with Children EMC 777

The Worm
A Stand-Up Book

1

Fold the green paper.

Cut slits as shown.

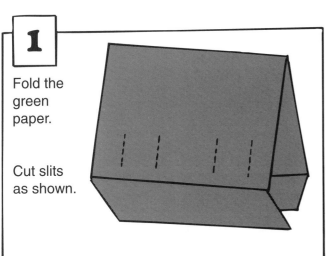

2

Fold the red paper.

Cut notches at each corner.

Lay out the red strip. Round corners on the first and last segments. Add details with felt pen.

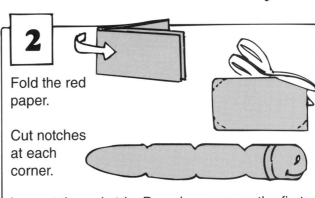

3

Fold the green paper into a stand-up position. Staple the bottom flaps.

Thread the worm through the slits in the green paper.

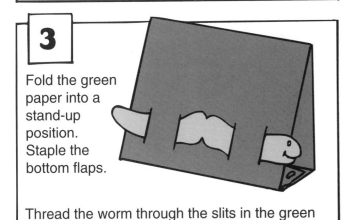

4

Decorate the writing form. Glue the story paper to the top of the stand.

For longer stories, cut writing paper the same size as the writing form. Staple pages to the green construction paper.

Literature Connections

The Big Fat Worm by Nancy Van Laan;
Alfred A. Knopf, 1987.

A rhythmic read-aloud describing what happens
when a big, fat bird tries to eat a big, fat worm.

Full Worm Moon by Margo Lemieux;
Tambourine Books, 1994.

An Algonquin family spends a cold night waiting
to see the earthworms dance.

National Worm Day by James Stevenson;
Greenwillow, 1990.

This book includes three funny stories about a
worm, a snail, and a rhinoceros.

Herman and Marguerite: An Earth Story by
Jay O'Callahan; Peachtree, 1996.

Four nonfiction reference books with good
information and doable activities.
Discovering Worms by Jennifer Coldrey;
Bookwright Press, 1986.

Earthworms by Terry Jennings; Gloucester
Press, 1988.

Earthworms, Dirt, and Rotten Leaves by
Molly McLaughlin; Atheneum, 1986.

Worms by Lynn Stone; Rourke, 1995.

Writing Connections

From a Worm's Point of View

What would it feel like to be a worm? Describe a
familiar item or an event from a worm's point of
view—a shoe, a fish hook, a rain storm, a shovel
digging.

Watching Worms

List all the adjectives and action words that you
can that describe the ways that worms look and
move. Use the words to create free verse poems
about worms.

Wet, wiggle

Smooth, squirm

Cold crawler — WORM

Why Worms?

Write an argument defending the rights of worms.
Refer to their contributions to life around them.

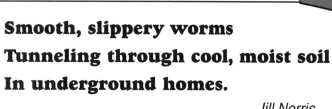

**Smooth, slippery worms
Tunneling through cool, moist soil
In underground homes.**

Jill Norris

Something More to Do...

A Worm Hunt

Suggest students have a worm hunt in their gardens or yards. They should dig up soil in several locations, search through it, and tally the number of worms found in the different locations.

Compare the information that different students collect.
- What locations do worms like best?
- How would you know?

Our Worm Count

6 worms in flower pot
4 worms in dry, sandy area
11 worms in shady area
21 worms

Listening for a Worm

Put a worm on a sheet of paper and listen carefully. You will hear little scratching noises. On almost every segment of an earthworm's body there are eight small bristles. These bristles help the worm to move along. The bristles make scratching noises on the paper.

Make a Home for Worms

Materials: glass jar, damp sand, damp soil, plastic, black paper, dead leaves, worms

Steps:
- Fill a jar with alternating layers of damp soil and damp sand.

- Put three worms and some dead leaves on top of the soil.

- Cover the jar with a piece of plastic. Make small holes in the plastic to let air in the jar so that the worms can breathe.

- Put a piece of black paper around the jar to keep the worms in the dark.

- One week later remove the paper. You will see that the worms have made burrows and that they have mixed up the layers of sand and soil. The leaves have been dragged down into the burrows.

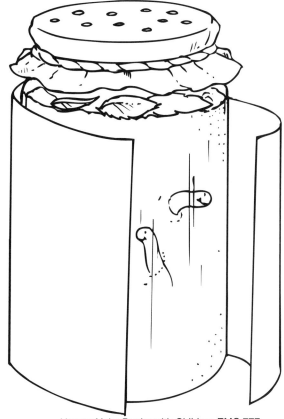

Garden ABCs
A Pull-Tab Book

Materials

Class book:

- seed packet and pull-tab patterns on pages 119 and 120
- 12" x 18" (30.5 x 45.5 cm) construction paper
- 5" x 8" (13 x 20 cm) writing paper
- scissors
- glue
- felt pens or crayons

1 Fill in the top box with the first letter and name of the plant.

Color the seed packet, label the type of seed.

Cut on the slit line.

2 On the pull-tab, draw the mature plant that will grow from the seed in the box.

3 Insert the pull-tab through the slit opening of the packet pattern.

Glue the packet pattern and the writing paper to the construction paper.

4 Put student packet pages in alphabetical order.

Bind the pages together with twine.

   How to Make Books with Children EMC 777

Literature Connections

***The Butterfly Seeds* by Mary Watson; Tambourine Books, 1995.**

When his family moves to America, Jake brings special seeds from his grandfather with him.

***The Emperor's Garden* by Ferida Wolff; Tambourine Books, 1994.**

The people of a poor village plan a garden for the emperor and argue about what to name the garden.

***A Garden for a Groundhog* by Lorna Balian; Abingdon Press, 1985.**

Farmer O'Leary tries to keep the groundhog from eating all the vegetables in his garden.

***Grandma's Garden* by Elaine Moore; Lothrop, Lee & Shepard, 1994.**

Kim helps her grandma plant her garden.

***In My Garden* by Ron Maris; Greenwillow, 1987.**

In this lift-the-flap book, a girl names the things in her garden.

***Jack's Garden* by Henry Cole; Greenwillow, 1995.**

Cumulative text tells what happens to Jack's garden after he plants his seeds.

***Pea Patch Jig* by Thatcher Hurd; Crown Publishers, 1986.**

The mouse family living at the edge of the garden has three adventures.

***Seeds* by George Shannon; Houghton Mifflin, 1994.**

Two friends move apart, but solve their loneliness with some seeds.

Writing Connections

Garden ABCs

Make a page for each letter of the alphabet.

All in a Row

You can plant anything that you want. Describe the garden that you would like to plant and why.

Rules for a Good Garden

Write a set of rules for new gardeners.

**It begins with some seeds
Gently placed in the ground
And ends up a garden,
Growing up all around.**

Jill Norris

Something More to Do...

Comparing Seeds

1. Buy several packets of seeds.

2. Take a few seeds from each packet and glue them to an index card or small paper plate.

3. Put the seed package with the remaining seeds into an envelope. Fasten the envelope to the back of the card or plate.

4. Show the seed card and ask for words that describe the seeds. Write the words around the seeds.

5. Predict what will grow when the seeds are planted.

6. Check the seed package to verify your predictions.

7. Plant some of each type of seeds and then write about their growth.

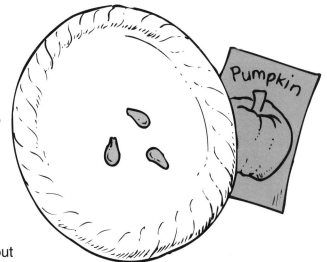

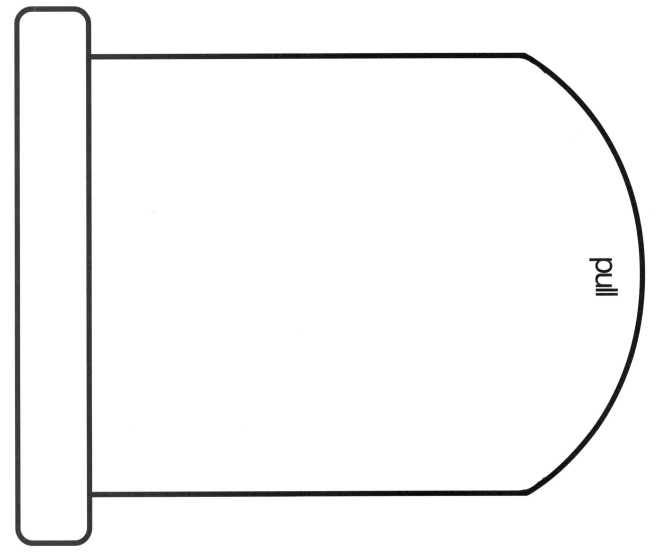

pull

is for

_____

cut

My Seed

_____

by

The Insect's Tale
A Pull-Tab Book

Class book:

- 12" x 18" (30.5 x 45.5 cm) construction paper
- 3" x 3" (7.5 x 7.5 cm) white paper squares
- reproducible forms on pages 123–124
- writing paper
- scissors, glue
- hole punch
- felt pens or crayons
- metal rings for binding
- X-acto® knife

1 Cut out the pull-tab form. Draw an insect in the center.

2 Color the jar.

Cut the slit with an X-acto® knife.

Slip the pull-tab through the slit.

3

Glue the outside edges of the jar paper to the construction paper.

Glue the writing paper next to the jar.

4 Create a cover from construction paper.

Glue on student pictures of their insects.

Punch holes through all layers. Insert metal rings.

Literature Connections

Amazing Anthony Ant by Lorna and Graham Philpot; Random House, 1994.

A maze, a song, a choice, and a search, all in the same book.

Benjamin's Bugs by Mary Morgan; Bradbury Press, 1994.

Benjamin Porcupine takes a walk with his mother and finds some bugs.

Insects Are My Life by Megan McDonald; Orchard Books, 1995.

In this story you will meet Amanda, a bug's best friend.

Leaving Home with a Pickle Jar by Barbara Dugan; Greenwillow, 1993.

Ernest P. takes his grasshopper with him when his family moves.

Step by Step by Diane Wolkstein; Morrow Junior Books, 1994.

Little ant shares a day with her friend, the grasshopper.

Two Bad Ants by Chris Van Allsburg; Houghton Mifflin, 1988.

Two ants experience a dangerous adventure.

Writing Connections

Down into an Ant Hill

Pretend you have shrunk to the size of an ant. Describe what you discover and experience when you crawl down into an ant hill.

A Nine-Foot-Long Ant

The ant has been spotted not far from your house. Measure to see how long that ant would be and then write about what could be done to find a good home for it.

Crawling,
Creeping,
Hopping,
Sleeping,
Digging,
Flying,
Biting,
Spying...
BUGS.

Jill Norris

Something More to Do...

Make a Bug Jar

1. Have each student draw a jar on a piece of white paper.

2. Students glue several beans or seeds in their "jars."

3. Then, students draw to change each bean into a bug.

4. Have students describe and name their bugs. Write or dictate these descriptions under the bug jar.

5. Take time to share the collections.

Write a Bug Poem

1. Read about real insects and spiders. Watch films and videos that show bugs in action.

2. Brainstorm words that describe things that bugs do. List the words on the chalkboard or a chart.

3. Have students choose 4–8 words from the list and write them one under the other on a thin piece of paper followed by the word BUGS.

4. After the poems are illustrated, laminate the strips of paper and use them as bookmarks.

fly
hop
jump
eat
flap
buzz
BUGS

Pull Tab Pattern

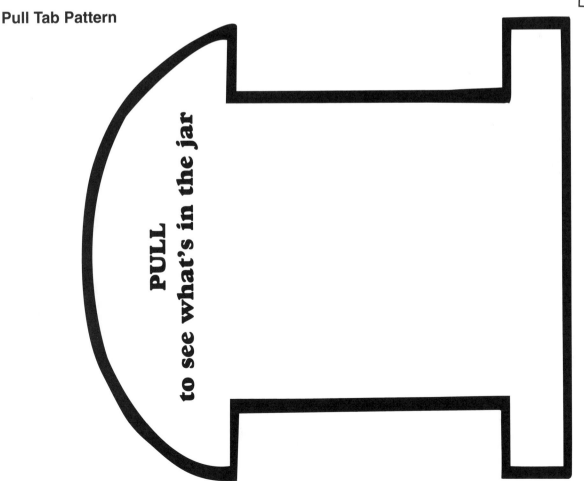

PULL
to see what's in the jar

The Mouse

A Pull-Tab Book

Materials

Class book:

- 12" x 18" (30.5 x 45.5 cm) construction paper
- reproducible forms on pages 127 and 128
- writing paper
- yellow construction paper scraps for cover
- scissors, X-acto® knife
- glue, hole punch
- felt pens or crayons
- a shoelace for binding

---

1 Cut out the pull-tab form. Color the mouse.

---

2 Color the picture. Is there anything waiting for mouse outside his hole?

Cut the slit with an X-acto® knife.

Slip the pull-tab through the slit.

3

Glue the outside edges of the paper to the construction paper.

Glue the writing paper next to the pull-tab paper.

---

4 Create a cover from construction paper.

Let students cut paper "swiss cheese" pieces for the cover.

Punch holes through all layers. Insert a shoelace.

Literature Connections

Mouse Paint and Mouse Count by Ellen Stoll Walsh; Harcourt Brace Jovanovich, 1992.

Two books that use mice as a focus for combining colors and for counting.

Owen by Kevin Henkes; Greenwillow, 1993.

Owen's parents try to get him to give up his favorite blanket.

Seven Blind Mice by Ed Young; Philomel Books, 1992.

Seven mice illustrate the importance of looking at the whole picture before making a judgment.

Town Mouse, Country Mouse retold by Jan Brett; G. P. Putnam's Sons, 1994.

The Town Mouse and the Country Mouse retold by Helen Craig; Candlewick Press, 1992.

Two retellings of the familiar folktale. Both have charming illustrations.

Writing Connections

How to Fool the Cat

Write a how-to guide for escaping from a cat.

Ten Ways to Eat Cheese

Create the latest recipe book for cheese-loving mice.

Mouse-Eye View

How would a mouse describe your closet?

Dear Friend,

Please get me some cheese.

I'm so easy to please.

Please bring it to me.

I'm starved as can be.

Cheddar, Jack, or even Swiss—

Any kind, you can't miss.

Please get me some cheese

I'm begging down on my knees.

Please get me some cheese.

Please, please, pretty please.

Signed,

Mousy Nibbles

Jill Norris

Something More to Do...

Torn Paper Mice

In *Mouse Count*, Ellen Stoll Walsh created her mice by tearing paper and adding legs, ears, tails, and eyes. Encourage students to create their own torn paper mice.

Materials:
- colored paper cut in 3" x 6" (7.5 x 18 cm) rectangles
- 2 2" (5 cm) black squares
- 1 1" (2.5 cm) black square
- hole punch, glue
- drinking straw and tape
- 6" (15 cm) piece of yarn

What to do:
1. Tear the edges of a piece of colored paper to form a body shape.
2. Round corners of black squares to make ears and nose. Glue on mouse.
3. Punch eye with the hole punch.
4. Punch a hole at the back and attach yarn for a tail.

How to use your mice:
- as counters in a math session
- as puppets (simply tape the torn paper mice to a craft stick or straw)
- as a border for a mouse bulletin board
- as bookmarks

Pull-Tab Pattern

PULL
to see who lives here

cut

How to Make Books with Children EMC 777

The Window

A Peek-Through Book

Materials

Individual books:

- 12" x 18" (30.5 x 45.5 cm) construction paper
- 9" x 12" (23 x 30.5 cm) white construction paper
- 3" x 3" (7.5 x 7.5 cm) white paper squares
- reproducible patterns on pages 131–132
- selection of paper scraps
- yarn for binding
- scissors, hole punch
- glue
- felt pens or crayons

1

Cut the window frame from the white paper.

2

Glue the top edge of the window frame to the large sheet of construction paper. Use paper scraps to create a scene. Slip the scene under the window and glue. Glue the window down.

3

Draw and color features on the outline of the person. Write what the person is saying in the speech bubble.

Glue this character and the speech bubble on the left side of the large paper.

4 Punch holes and lace with yarn.

Place all layers together. Create a cover with each student providing a miniature window by drawing a picture on the small white squares.

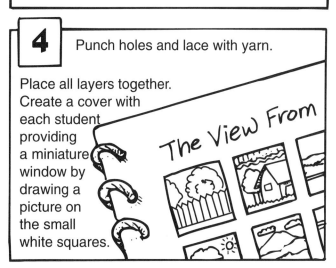

The View From

How to Make Books with Children EMC 777

Literature Connections

From My Window by Olive Wong; Silver Press, 1995.

A little boy tells about the things that he sees from his window.

Let There Be Light by James Cross Giblin; Thomas Y. Crowell, 1988.

This reference book surveys the development of windows from prehistory to present.

Window by Jeannie Baker; Greenwillow, 1991.

A wordless storybook shows the same scene at different times chronicling the changes in a community.

A Window of Time by Audrey O. Leighton; Nadja Publishing, 1995.

In this story about a grandfather and his grandson, Grandpa says that memories are like a window of time.

Writing Connections

What Is Outside Your Window?

Show the view from a window in your home. Does it change with the seasons? What does it look like during a full moon?

What Is a Window?

Describe the window in physical terms and then use metaphors and similes to describe a window and its function.

The window is a crack in the protective armor of family. Through the window you first glimpse the world outside the cozy warmth of your mother's embrace.

A Window on Time

Imagine yourself in a different country or a different time period. Describe what is outside your window.

Note: Use this topic as an assessment tool when you complete a study of a country or an era in history.

The Magic Window

The window at the back of the house looks over a lake and a meadow, but when you lift the bottom part to let the air in amazing things happen...

I'm on the inside looking out.
You're on the outside looking in.
I'll wave to you. You wave to me.
We'll nod to each other and grin.

Jill Norris

Something More to Do...

The Seasons from My Window

Describe the view from your window during different seasons. How does the view change? What specific differences can you name? Have students draw and write about the view they see. Collect all the fall descriptions in a fall window book, the winter descriptions in a winter book, etc., or have students include all of their different views in a single book.

Different People See Different Views

Use the window to demonstrate point of view. Have several people look out the same window and note the different things that they see. For example, a student, a teacher, and a custodian looking at a view of the playground:

student —
The second grade's outside. Look at Sammy swing! I can't wait to get outside and fly high.

teacher —
Oh dear, we need to review the rules for the climbing structure. That little girl could be hurt.

custodian —
The wind last night blew the tumbleweeds into the schoolyard. I'm going to need to clean them up.

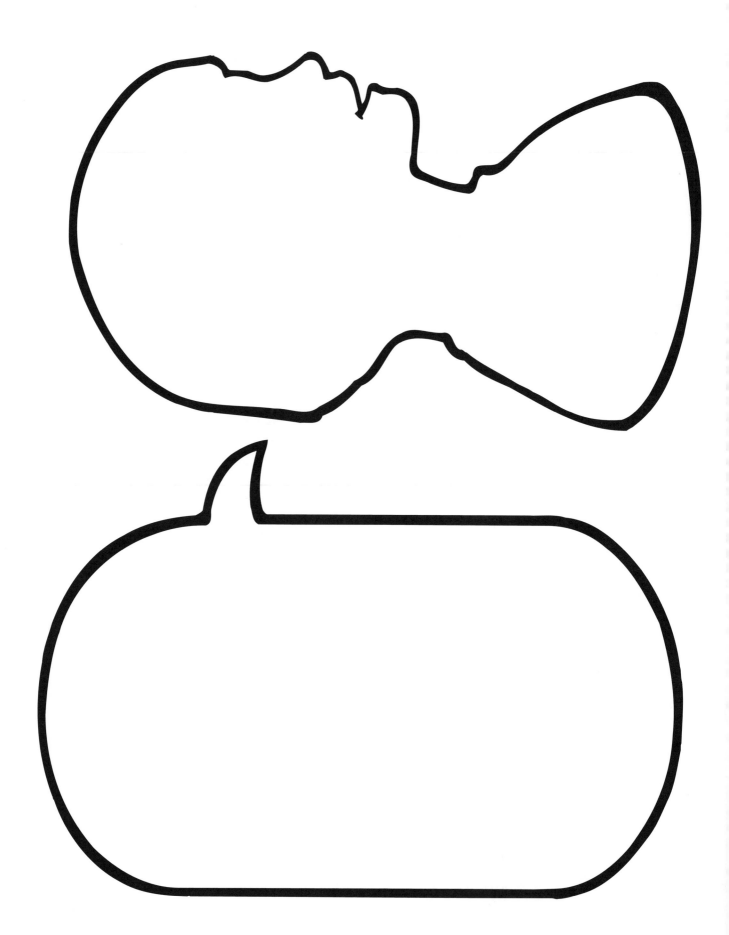

How to Make Books with Children EMC 777

The Riddle-Bag Book

A Paper-Bag Book

Materials

Class book:

- paper lunch bags
- writing form on page 136
- "surprises" to place in the bag
- scissors, glue
- felt pens or crayons
- hole punch
- 2 sheets of tagboard cut 6" x 11" (15 x 28 cm) to use as covers
- a metal ring

---

1 Write a riddle on the writing form. Glue the form to the bag.

2 Tuck the surprise in the bag.

3 Decorate a cover for the book.

4 Place all layers together. Punch a hole in the top corner and insert ring.

Literature Connections

The Gumdrop Tree by Elizabeth Spurr;
Hyperion Books, 1994.

When her father gives her a bag of gumdrops, a little girl decides to plant them instead of eating them.

Night of the Moonjellies by Mark Shasha;
Simon & Schuster, 1992.

Mark collects bits of glass smoothed by the tides and a piece of something that feels like jelly.

The Paper Bag Prince by Colin Thompson; Alfred A. Knopf, 1992.

An old man moves into an abandoned train and watches as nature reclaims the area around a junkyard.

The Paper Bag Princess by Robert N. Munsch; Annick Press, 1989.

A fairy tale about an unusual princess.

Writing Connections

The Riddle-Bag Book

Write good clues to help people guess what's in your paper bag.

The Surprise

The bag on the table wiggled and bulged out on one side. What could be in it? How did it get there? What will happen to it?

The Mystery Bag

Jonathan put a paper bag over his head, and when he did, something very unusual happened...

Is it heavy? Is it light?

It is black or red or white?

Is it something good to eat?

Do you wear it on your feet?

Is it alive? Will it grow?

Tell me so that I will know.

What is in the bag??

Jill Norris

Something More to Do...

Creating Rhyming Riddles

Hink-Pinks
A hink-pink is two one-syllable words that rhyme and answer a riddle. Here are some examples:

What do you call the person who provides security for a parking lot? *a yard guard*

What do you call an overweight feline? *a fat cat*

What do you call a sunless morning and afternoon? *a gray day*

What noise does a sick mouse make? *a weak squeak*

What did the fish do when it swallowed the worm? *It ate bait*

What do you call a playground without lights? *a dark park*

What do you call Sylvester Stallone's automobile? *a star car*

What do you call a paper bag full of pretzels and candy? *a snack sack*

After sharing several hink-pinks with your students, work together to write a new one. Follow this format:
1. List rhyming words. The more rhyming "families" you create, the better.
    all ball brawl call crawl doll fall tall small stall wall
2. Choose two words from the list (usually one adjective and one noun).
    tall wall
3. Write a question that can be answered with the two words.
    What would you need to keep a giraffe in a pen?

When the class seems comfortable with the format, turn them loose to write their own.

Extension
Move on to hinky-pinky riddles (two-syllable rhyming pairs) and hinkity-pinkity riddles (three-syllable rhyming pairs) with groups that are more sophisticated.

Hinky-Pinky Riddles
What do you call the label on a letter bag?
> *a mailbag nametag*

What do you call an alligator with a skateboard?
> *a gator skater*

What do you call a cowboy who has spent the summer in the sun?
> *a suntanned cowhand*

Hinkity-Pinkity Riddles
What might you call a used piano?
> *a secondhand baby grand*

What do you call a swamp creature with a protest sign?
> *an alligator agitator*

What do you call a story about two bunnies who lived happily ever after?
> *a cottontail fairy tale*

The Hat

A Pull-Up Book

Class book:

- 6" x 18" (15 x 45.5 cm) strip of white construction paper
- 9" x 12" (23 x 30.5 cm) colored construction paper
- 2" x 9" (5 x 23 cm) strip of construction paper
- reproducible patterns on page 140
- scissors, glue
- felt pens or crayons

1

Fold the white construction paper over 7" (18 cm). Fold it back in half.

$3\frac{1}{2}$"

2

Glue the folded paper to the colored paper.

Fold the writing form and glue it into the fold.

3

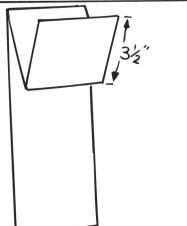

Draw a hat on the folded paper and its wearer below.

Write a description of the hat.

Glue the *Hats, Hats* form next to the pull-up.

4

Assemble student stories and let students design a cover.

Staple the pages together and cover with the strip of paper.

Literature Connections

Anno's Hat Tricks by Akihiro Nozaki; Philomel Books, 1984.

Readers use logic to solve problems with colored hats.

Caps for Sale by Esphr Slobodkina; Harper & Row, 1940.

Monkeys cause problems for a poor peddler.

This Is the Hat by Nancy Van Laan; Little, Brown, 1992.

When the wind blows a hat away, it becomes a home for a spider, a mouse, and other creatures before returning to its rightful owner.

A Man and His Hat by Letitia Parr; Philomel Books, 1989.

An old man searches for his missing hat.

Martin's Hats by Joan W. Blos; William Morrow, 1984.

Martin wears a different hat for every adventure that he has.

Writing Connections

Whose Hat Is That?

What kind of hat would you wear if you were a clown, a cowboy, an artist, the president? Use descriptive language to tell about it.

Choose Me

Imagine that you are a hat on the shelf of a hat store. What will you do to be chosen by the customer who just came in the store?

I Love My Hat!

Write about the hat you would most like to have. Tell how you would feel wearing it.

Tall ones...
Small ones...
Clown ones...
Brown ones...
Flower ones...
Shower ones...

Sun ones...
Fun ones...
Hard ones...
Guard ones...
Ball ones...
Doll ones...

That's hats!!

Jill Norris

Something More to Do...

Design a Hat with a Special Purpose

Many people wear hats to help them or to protect them in some way.

I'm going to make a hat that will take pictures of all the people that I meet.

1. Have students think of something special that a hat could do and then design a hat for that purpose.

2. Designers should draw a diagram showing their hat and its unusual feature(s).

3. The diagrams might be used as part of an "ad campaign" to promote the new chapeaux. Eager entrepreneurs may even make hat models.

What a Hat!

Decorating hats is always fun. Use the hats to create a three dimensional bulletin board— **Hats Off to You**—saluting student accomplishments.

1. Provide a variety of craft materials, almost anything that you have in your cupboard. Then challenge students to create a hat. For young children you may need to provide a base (extra large coffee filters or paper plates) to decorate. Older students will enjoy the challenge of creating their own base.

2. Attach the hats to the bulletin board. Don't pin them flat. Even the plainest hat has character when it is given dimension.

3. Write one special achievement for each student on a strip of paper and add these to the bulletin board.

Hats

Hats

Hats

by:

How to Make Books with Children EMC 777

The Gift
A Pull-Down Book

Class book:

- 5 1/2" x 18" (16.25 x 45.5 cm) white construction paper
- 12" x 12" (30.5 x 30.5 cm) colored construction paper
- reproducible forms on page 144
- scissors, glue, hole punch
- felt pens or crayons
- ribbon for binding
- string for the gift tag

1

Fold the white construction paper to look like a box.

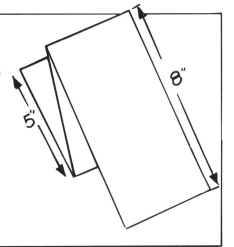

2

Glue this box to the colored construction paper.

Design a fancy wrapping paper.

3

Write about what is in the box. Glue it next to the box.

Pull down the gift box and draw what is inside.

Add the bow and gift tag.

4

Assemble all student pages together with a cover.

Punch holes and bind together with real ribbon.

Literature Connections

Birthday Present **by Catherine Stock;**
Bradbury Press, 1991.

A boy must take a gift that his mother chose to his
friend's birthday party.

Birthday Presents **by Cynthia Rylant;**
Orchard Books, 1987.

In this poignant story, parents describe the
birthdays that their five-year-old has had.

Gifts **by Jo Ellen Bogart and Barbara Reid;**
Scholastic, 1994.

This question-answer rhyme describes the gifts
that a grandma brings back from her journeys.

The Giving Tree **by Shel Silverstein; Harper**
& Row, 1964.

A classic story of the unselfish gifts of love that a
tree gives to a boy.

Lily and the Present **by Christine Ross;**
Houghton Mifflin, 1992.

Lily tries to find the perfect gift for her baby brother.

Writing Connections

A Special Gift

What's in this birthday box?

How to Wrap a Gift

Explain how you would wrap an unusual gift.

From Aunt Sylvie

Aunt Sylvie always gives unusual presents. Tell
what she gave you for your birthday this year
and how you reacted.

It's fun to get a gift
No matter what the day.
But the best gift of all,
Is one you give away.

Jill Norris

Something More to Do...

A Gift of Love

1. Encourage your students to think of gifts they can give that cannot be purchased.

A hug... A smile... A clean room... A chore done without asking

2. Create a bulletin board of these special "Giving Tree" gifts.
   - Have students draw their gifts on leaf-shaped pieces of paper.
   - Create a bare branch on a bulletin board and tape the leaves to the branch.
   - Add tiny bows or flowers as the branches are filled with gifts of love to celebrate the spirit of giving.

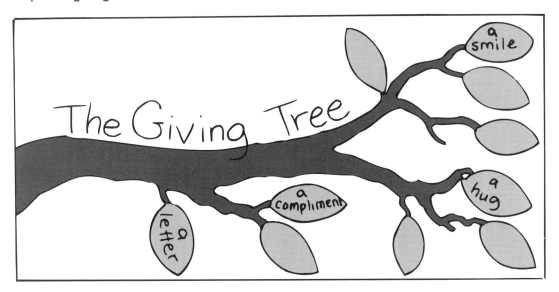

What Would They Like?

1. Ask each student to select a favorite literary character.

2. Ask students to choose a gift that the character would like and tell why they chose that particular gift.

3. Share your ideas. What kind of a party do you think Curious George would have? How about Ramona? Wilbur? The BFG?

I think Wilbur would like corn as a gift.

The Gift

The Sun Through the Window

A Wheel Book

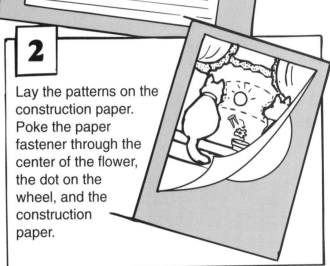

Materials

Class book:

- book patterns on pages 147–148
- 12" x 18" (39.5 x 45.5 cm) construction paper
- writing paper
- paper fastener
- scissors
- felt pens or crayons
- glue

1 Color and cut out the wheel and window patterns.

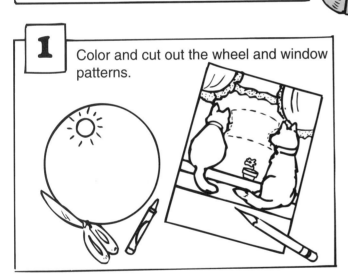

2 Lay the patterns on the construction paper. Poke the paper fastener through the center of the flower, the dot on the wheel, and the construction paper.

3 Glue the window pattern along the top and bottom edge.

Glue the writing paper below.

4 Collect all the student stories and bind together. Decorate the cover with a crayon resist illustration.

Literature Connections

Dad and Me in the Morning by Patricia Lakin;
A. Whitman, 1994.

A deaf boy and his dad share a sunrise at the
beach.

The First Strawberries retold by Joseph
Bruchac; Dial Books, 1993.

A Cherokee story about how the sun created the
first strawberries.

How Snowshoe Hare Rescued the Sun retold
by Emery Bernard; Holiday House, 1993.

An Arctic tale about the long dark days of winter.

The Sun's Day by Mordicai Gerstein; Harper
& Row, 1989.

This picture book provides an hour-by-hour
description of activities as the sun rises, moves
through the sky, and then sets.

Sun Up by Alvin Tresselt; Lothrop, Lee &
Shepard, 1991.

The sun lights up a farm morning.

Hot spot
In the sun.

Cool pool
We'll have fun.

Jill Norris

Writing Connections

The Sun Through the Window

Watch the sun from your window at different times
in the day. Describe the way it looks and tell what
you see happening.

No Sun

What would happen if the sun didn't rise one
morning? Write a story that explains what you
think.

Sun Rhymes

Brainstorm words that describe the sun. Use
them as you write simple poems.

> Radiant yellow, shining bright
> Rising sun turns off the night.

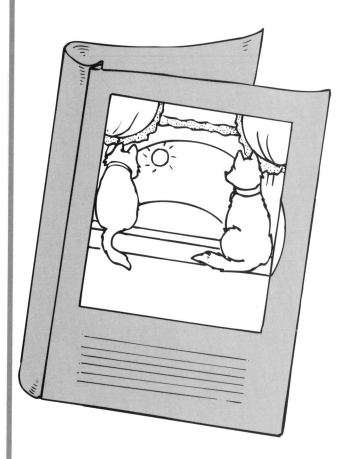

Something More to Do...

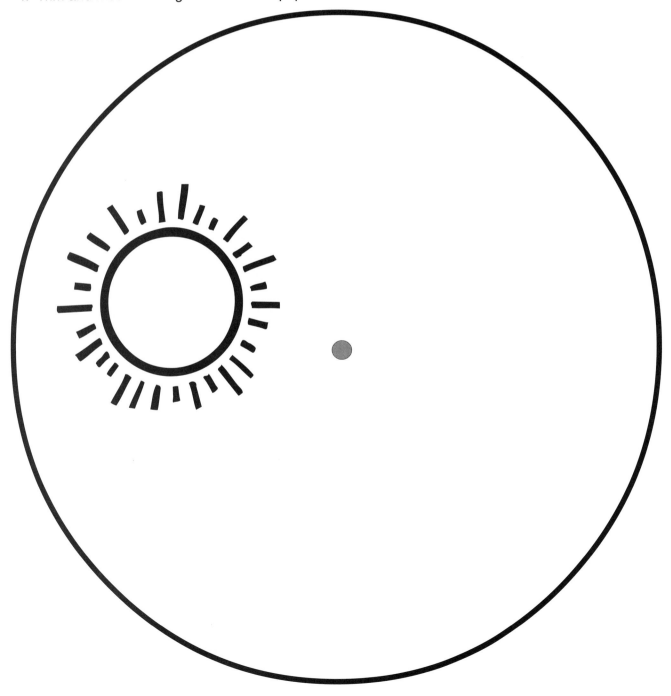

Crayon Resist Sun

Brighten your classroom with colorful suns.

Materials:
brightly colored construction paper, scissors, white drawing paper, crayons, yellow and orange watercolor paint, paint brush, water

1. With a light, bright crayon, draw a circle on a piece of white drawing paper.
2. Use several more bright crayons to create a sun face. Add several layers of rays and facial features.
3. Now add the background color with a watercolor wash.
4. Trim and mount on bright construction paper.

Window Pattern

How to Make Books with Children EMC 777

The Castle
A Double-Hinged Book

Materials

Class book:

- 1 sheet of 12" x 14" (30.5 x 35.5 cm) tagboard
- 1 sheet of 10" x 14" (25.5 x 35.5 cm) tagboard
- 2 strips of 2" x 10" (5 x 25.5 cm) paper
- 8 1/2" x 11" (21.5 x 28 cm) writing paper
- 6" x 6" (15 x 15 cm) black paper
- scissors, stapler
- felt pens

Individual books:

Use the pattern on page 152.

---

1 Cut the tagboard into the castle shape.

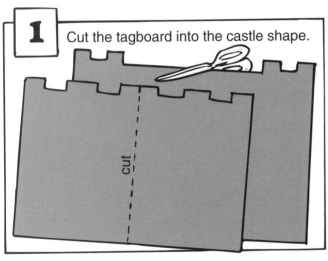

cut

2

Use felt pen to create the block shapes on the castle wall.

Cut the black paper to make a door and windows.

3

Staple the front cover on the left and right side. Cover the sides with strips of paper.

4

Castle Stories

Room 6

Staple student stories inside.

Literature Connections

Castle by David Macaulay; Houghton Mifflin, 1977.

This book includes the planning and construction of a typical fourteenth century castle.

The Castle Builder by Dennis Nolan; Macmillan, 1987.

A young boy builds a sand castle on the beach.

Henry and Mudge and the Long Weekend by Cynthia Rylant; Bradbury Press, 1992.

Henry and Mudge are bored until they begin building a castle.

The Prince Who Wrote a Letter by Ann Love; Child's Play Limited, 1992.

When Prince Paul writes a letter, two kings from two different castles almost have a war.

Stephen Biesty's Cross-Sections—Castle by Stephen Biesty; Dorling Kindersley, 1994.

Mr. Biesty's drawings and informative text show the story of life in a medieval castle.

The Story of a Castle by John S. Goodall; Margaret K. McElderry Books, 1986.

A wordless picture book that traces life in a typical English castle from its construction in 1170 until it was opened to the public as a museum in 1970.

Writing Connections

Life in a Castle

Pretend that you are a page working in the castle. Describe your life and tell how it is different from the lives of the brave knights and beautiful princesses around you.

The Haunted Castle

A ghost lives within the castle walls. Write a thrilling saga to tell about the ghost's adventures.

A Fairy Tale

Read a variety of fairy tales and list the elements that they have in common. Then write your own fairy tale. Make sure that it includes the elements common to most fairy tales.

Imagine walls of stone,
A moat circling 'round,
Turrets standing tall,
And dungeons underground,
A drawbridge and a lookout,
A great hall and a king:
Living in a castle
Would be an awesome thing.

Jill Norris

Something More to Do...

Build a Castle

1. Encourage students to use boxes or building blocks to build a castle. The castle may be a class, small group, or individual project.

2. Have the builders draw up plans and describe the building process.

3. Then have them imagine who lives in the castle and what is going on inside the walls. Write about these characters.

Change the Setting of a Familiar Story

1. Tell a familiar story such as *Little Red Riding Hood* or *Goldilocks and the Three Bears.*

2. Have students imagine that the setting of the story was a castle. Think about how the story would change.

3. Create puppets for the characters in the story and act out the story with the castle backdrop.

4. Rewrite the story in the castle setting.

       How to Make Books with Children EMC 777

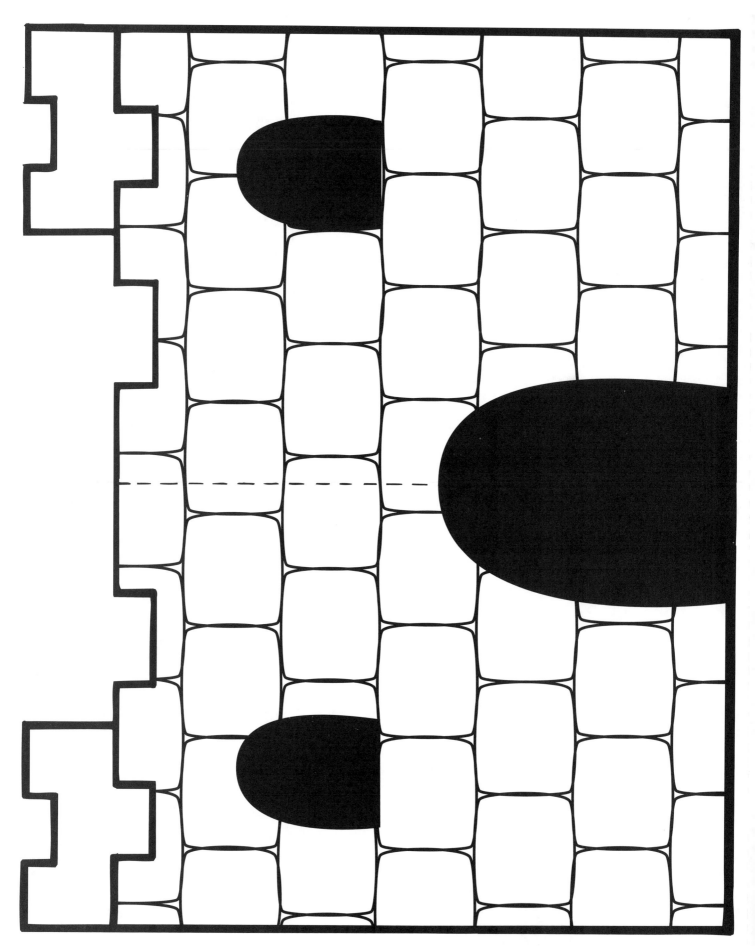

How to Make Books with Children EMC 777

The Cloud

A Double-Hinged Book

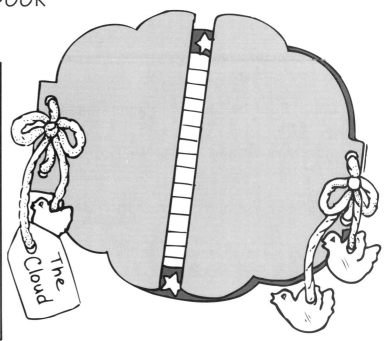

1

Cut the silver and the blue tagboard using the cloud shape pattern on page 156.

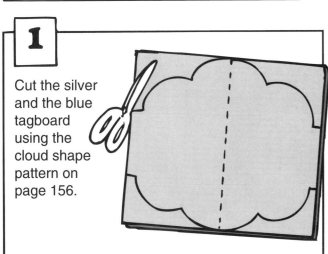

2 Collect student stories and staple them to the blue tagboard. Add the gold star stickers.

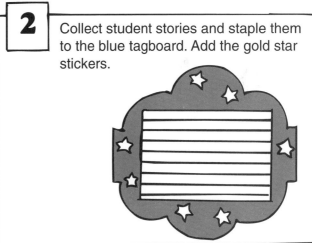

3 Cut the silver cloud in half. Put the silver cloud parts on top.

Punch holes on each side. Thread yarn through and tie in a bow.

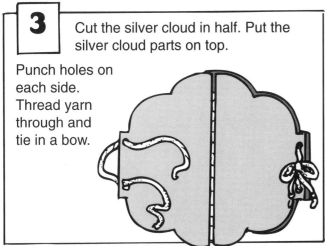

4 Tie little birds and a story tag on the strings.

Literature Connections

The Cloud by Deborah Logan Ray; Harper & Row, 1984.

A little girl and her mother hike up a mountain and walk through a cloud.

The Cloud Book by Tomie de Paola; Holiday House, 1975.

Learn about ten different kinds of clouds in this nonfiction book.

Cloud Nine by Norman Silver; Clarion Books, 1995.

Armstrong escapes the noise of his house and builds a ladder to the clouds.

Cloudy with a Chance of Meatballs by Judith Barrett; Atheneum, 1978.

Some very unusual weather is part of this story.

Like Butter on Pancakes by Jonathan London; Viking, 1995.

A farm morning is described in beautiful similes.

> **Wispy threads of white**
> **Against a sky of blue**
> **Or puffs of squishy gray**
> **Looking down on you.**
>
> **My father looks up and says,**
> **"There's moisture in the air."**
> **But I see ballerinas**
> **Dancing without a care.**
>
> *Jill Norris*

Writing Connections

Cloud Pictures

Describe the forms you see in the clouds. Use the words to write a free verse poem.

In the Clouds

Imagine that you were a tiny drop of water in a cloud; describe your journey to earth and back to the cloud.

Behind the Cloud

What would you find if you could get behind that great black cloud?

Something More to Do...

Understanding Condensation

Water vapor in the air condenses to form clouds and sometimes rain. Demonstrate this condensation in your classroom.

1. The steam from a boiling kettle forms as water vapor escapes from the hot water inside the kettle and meets the colder air outside. Tiny drops of liquid water condense from the vapor and join together until they are big enough for you to see as clouds of steam.

2. Put a spoon in a refrigerator or freezer for several hours. Hold the spoon in the steam from the tea kettle; the water vapor will condense and drip off. Safety tip: Make sure that you wear an oven mitt on the hand holding the spoon.

Heat from the sun makes the liquid water in oceans, rivers, and lakes evaporate just like the heating element under the tea kettle did. Water vapor rises into the air. At very high levels, the air is too cold to hold all the vapor and the water droplets begin to condense from the vapor. Clouds begin to form. The droplets stay in the clouds until they get too heavy to hang in the air. When that happens, they fall as rain.

Cloud Observations

1. Make daily cloud observations. Describe the appearance of the clouds and the weather conditions in a notebook.

2. Read about the different types of clouds. Identify the clouds that you have described in your observation notebook.

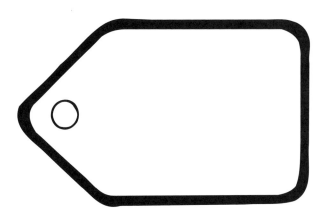

Bird Pattern

Title Tag Pattern

How to Make Books with Children EMC 777

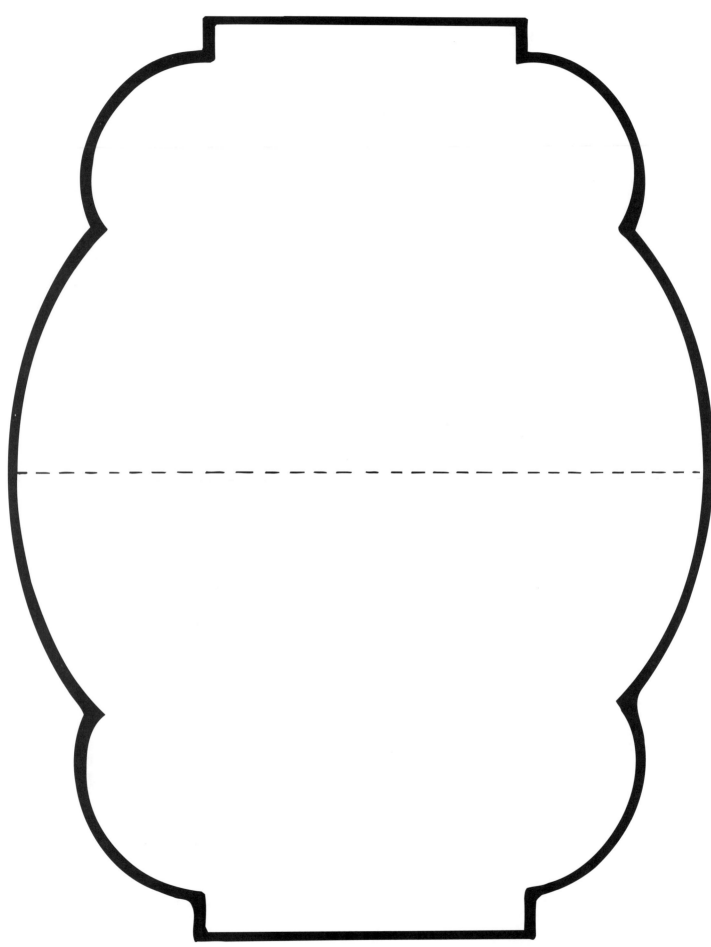

How to Make Books with Children EMC 777

The Penguin

A Double-Hinged Book

1 Color and cut out the penguin. Paste it to one of the blue sheets of paper to create the back cover.

2 Cut the other sheet of blue paper in a wavy or jagged line. Cut the writing paper to match this shape. Then cut the blue sheet down the center.

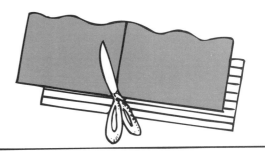

3 Staple the writing papers and the left cover sheet to the back cover. Staple the right-hand cover to the back cover.

Fold penguin's wings over the covers. Tuck a baby penguin under the wing.

4 Print the title on the cover panels.

Cover the staples with folded strips of blue paper.

Literature Connections

Cinderella Penguin or The Little Glass Flipper; Viking, 1992.

A new version of the fairy tale *Cinderella*.

Little Penguin by Patrick Benson; Philomel Books, 1990.

A little Adelie penguin is unhappy because she is so small compared to Emperor penguins.

Penguin Pete, Ahoy by Marcus Pfister; North-South Books, 1993.

Penguin Pete meets a mouse and learns about life onboard a ship.

The Penguin's Tale by Audrey Wood; Harcourt Brace Jovanovich, 1989.

Little Penguin searches for fun in his snowy polar world.

Tacky the Penguin by Helen Lester; Houghton Mifflin, 1988.

Tacky doesn't fit in with his graceful companions.

Writing Connections

A Day in the Life of a Penguin

What would it be like to live on the icy polar snow? Write about what you think a penguin's day would be like.

A Penguin Counting Book

One sleek penguin swimming in the sea.
Two waddling fathers heading to the sea.
Three fluffy babies sliding on the ice.

A Penguin Folk Tale

Substitute a penguin for a character in your favorite folk tale and retell it.

> *The Three Little Penguins*
> *Little Red Riding Penguin*
> *Goldilocks and the Three Penguins*

Rows of black and white,
Dressed in formal attire—
Penguins on parade,
An antarctic choir.

Jill Norris

A Close Look at Ice

You will need:
- a small bottle made of glass or thick plastic — about the same size as the bottles used for food coloring
- aluminum foil
- water
- freezer

What to do:

1. Fill the bottle to the brim with water. Make a loose-fitting cap out of aluminum foil.

2. Put the bottle in the freezer and leave it until the water has frozen hard.

3. Remove the bottle from the freezer and notice what has happened to the aluminum foil cap. (The ice pushed it up.)

How it works:

Ice takes up more space than the water that froze to make it. Pipes may burst in the winter. The water inside them expands as it freezes and forces the joints apart or makes the pipes split.

More to do:

Float an ice cube in a glass of water. What will happen when the ice cube melts? Will the glass overflow? Watch and see.

(When the ice cube melts, the level of water in the glass stays about the same. This is because the water from the ice takes up less space than the ice itself.)

Penguin Chick Pattern

How to Make Books with Children EMC 777

How to Make Books with Children EMC 777